# All the Dogs We've Loved Before & Cats We Have Served

## Diana Lariviere

CAWLAR Publications
www.cawlar.ca

All the Dogs We've Loved Before & Cats We Have Served
© 2022 Diana Lariviere

First CAWLAR Publications Edition April 2022

Front cover photo: The author with her beloved brother, Edgar Lariviere.
Front cover photo © CAWLAR Publications
Interior photos © individual photographers, CAWLAR Publications, needpix.com,
and iStock (Bat-Animal 1176923712 Connie Pinson)
Cover Design © 2022 Crowe Creations
Interior design by Crowe Creations
crowecreations.ca
Text set in Garamond; headings in Clarity Gothic SF

CAWLAR Publications
ISBN: 978-1-7781244-0-2

To all of the amazing animals that bring — or have brought — such joy to our lives and to the lives of our family and friends.
May their animal spirits live forever in our hearts.

To my parents, Marjorie Hansen and Solomon Lariviere,
who impressed upon me
a deep respect for all living creatures.

# Table of Contents

There's no doubt about it. Animals are beautiful and entertaining. They certainly deserve much more respect and protection than is generally accorded them, both in law and in practice.

# Prologue

Animals have always been a part of me. They inhabit my inner spirit.

My earliest childhood memories are of my mom dressing me in a snowsuit and my dad bundling me up in blankets and lifting me into the canvas "basket" of his dog sled.

The lead dog, Blacky, was the one that Dad trusted to keep the team's pace strong and steady — as well as safe from air holes in the ice — as we travelled across the frozen lake and back again.

The surrounding silence was comforting — the *swish-swish* of the runners across the snow, birds twittering, subtle sounds from unknown

sources and the dogs happily panting. On the return trip that was often at dusk, the occasional howl of wolves echoed off in the distance. When the wolves howled, the dogs would run faster and faster to get home, back to the comfort of their shelters and the meal they knew awaited them. That speed could have had some very unfortunate consequences but my dad — supplemented by Blacky's leadership skill — had amazing control over the team to take us safely home.

Thanks to my dad, I grew up with virtually no fear of wild animals — although I was taught a healthy respect for them and the need to not encroach upon their space. There were always four-legged critters to keep me occupied: rabbits, a raccoon, a squirrel, birds, chickens (among them, lots of roosters), as well as dogs and cats. Dad had incredible patience and gentleness when it came to animals. He could entice them to do just about anything. More about those adventures later.

As I grew into a walking, talking, curious child wanting to play outside, Mom was concerned about my taking off to the lake or, worse, being carried off into the surrounding forest by one of the many wild animals that always hovered unseen. As a safety measure, Mom gifted me with a black lab mix. We called her Bunny because it seemed that when I called my pet bunny, the dog would come running, so the name stuck to the dog as well.

Regrettably, I don't remember a lot about Bunny and her exploits, but I do remember that we were close pals. As gentle as Bunny was with me, the Fates forbid if anyone or anything came anywhere near me. Then the growling and barking would start. To Mom's relief, if she couldn't find me or if I chose not to answer when she called (which happened more often than not), Bunny would prance out of our hiding place, giving us both up. My mom knew I was safe with Bunny as my ever-present companion. Later in life, I used this same technique when I couldn't find my husband, William, on our hobby farm.

There was also Minew, my very first cat (with six more to come later in life). Again, my memories are faint, but I do remember that she slept on my bed, cuddled up, purred very loudly and kept me company. As I recall, Minew didn't seem to object to prancing around in doll clothes. Insofar as I was concerned, Minew's greatest claim to fame in my memory was when a teensy field mouse decided to jump on the bed and I awoke with a fright. The mouse lost that battle.

Since then, a fur-baby of one type or another has always been a part of my life. Truth be told, I can't imagine not having a warm, cuddly companion or two to brighten my days and adore me as only a beloved pet can. Each furry companion has been unique, with its own individual traits and personality, each distinguishing itself from the rest. I cherished each one for different reasons. I stood by them when the time came for them to cross over the rainbow bridge. Although I suffered deeply at every loss and miss them still, I remember each one with love. They are forever tucked away in my heart.

These are their stories. I hope you enjoy reading them as much as I enjoyed writing them.

If you have been rewarded with an animal companion, these stories will delight you as you recall or reflect upon your own pet's behaviours that bring joy to your heart. If the unconditional loyalty of a pet has not yet found its way into your life, these stories may inspire you to contact a local shelter or animal rescue group to adopt a lifelong friend.

DL
2022

# All the Dogs We've Loved Before

Diana Lariviere

# Digger

The very first dog I remember with any clarity is Digger (so-called for reasons the name accurately suggests). Digger spent most of his "puppy" time with me. His fur was snowy white and he had piercing green eyes that reflected awesome intelligence that would serve him well throughout his lifetime.

Unlike my siblings, whose huskies were their mode of transport to school, I arrived on the scene when my parents had a house in town, so I was relegated to the boredom of walking to school. Digger had to join my dad's sleigh team and work for his keep; but the bond between us never diminished.

All of the husky-sleigh dogs were kept together in an outdoor area well away from the tourists and curious onlookers. Each dog had its own doghouse, with a good thick supply of hay that was refreshed regularly to keep them clean and comfortable. A heavy leather cover hung over the door to keep out the wind, rain and snow (or sun), while allowing the dogs to enter/exit at will.

The dogs were tied, but my dad fashioned an ingenious T-bar arrangement out of compatible-sized logs. The upright log was wedged well into the

6

ground, with a lighter-weight top bar that was screwed into the top of the upright log. This allowed the upper lighter-weight bar to swivel unimpaired. A chain suitable to the dog's size was attached to one end of the upper swivel bar, with a weight attached to the other end of that upper bar.

As difficult as this is to explain, each dog had relatively free movement without getting tangled around anything nor being able to reach any of the other dogs. It also allowed each dog to reach the water in the nearby stream to drink anytime it was thirsty — and to relieve him/herself away from the doghouse.

What must also be kept in mind is that this was a working team that ventured out on a regular basis so, when they were tied, they were tired and ecstatic to have some down time to eat, sleep and roll contentedly in the grass.

Digger quite enjoyed his job as a sled dog and spending time with his canine companions, but he seemed to know when I was home — even though the house and the lodge were a considerable distance away. To my dad's frustration, Digger was one dog — and the only one — that consistently managed to get loose.

One day, Digger suddenly appeared while I was playing outdoors with various other animals. Some of the tourists standing nearby drew in a breath as they witnessed this large dog approaching. But Digger was a gentle spirit despite his muscular build. Digger simply came over to me, sniffed my hair, sniffed each of the other critters and threw himself down beside me to observe the goings on in silence.

Digger was an exceptional judge of character and, although he was a gentle soul, his intense stare could be enough to deter even the biggest, meanest human from approaching. Digger was also adept at picking up on body language and other invisible cues that emanated from the people he did like … and one of those was my mom.

As it happened, my mom had developed a deep-rooted dislike for one particular club member. Truth to tell, none of us liked this fellow — whom we will call "Mr. Q". Even the other club members found him objectionable.

Mr. Q was one of those stereotypical characters right out of a really bad movie. Mr. Q never smiled, never had anything positive to say and complained about virtually everything. Mr. Q hated people, animals and, methinks, life in general. He must have been a real joy to live with.

To be fair, Mr. Q was particularly meticulous with his appearance. Although he was not particularly tall and a bit on the heavy side, he always wore a neatly pressed shirt and tie, suit pants and well-shined shoes. His hair and small moustache were always neatly trimmed — with his trendy glasses perched securely on his nose.

My mom, who was always happy and smiling, had little in common with the obnoxious Mr. Q. One day, Mr. Q drove up and, as soon as he got out of his car, started in on my mom about something — probably Digger's being loose in the yard.

Digger must have picked up on my mom's vibe and meandered menacingly over to Mr. Q who froze on the spot, his hands gripping the top of the car door, his knuckles turning white. As Digger sniffed, Mr. Q just stared ahead, frozen with fear and not saying another word. Digger then took a walk around the car and went back to Mr. Q, whereupon Digger lifted his leg and, with perfect aim, managed to pee all the way down Mr. Q's pant leg, from the knee onto the shiny shoe.

While my dad stood horrified at what had just happened, my mother's hand instinctively went to her mouth, stifling a laugh.

The deed done, Digger casually walked away, sat down under a tree and began grooming himself — but never taking his eye off his prey. Without a word, Mr. Q got back into the car and drove away.

Good boy, Digger!

# Ferdie

Ferdie was a Dachshund (or, sausage dog) with the usual long body, short legs, fetching eyes and an exceptionally vibrant personality. William and I were Ferdie's third family, but the route by which Ferdie came to us is very interesting.

I've not been able to confirm all the facts concerning the reasons for Ferdie's initial acquisition by my mother-in-law, Ann; however, Ferdie was reportedly saved from rather dismal circumstances.

As the story goes, Ferdie started out life as the companion to the butcher's wife — until the local butcher discovered that his wife was involved in an illicit affair. In retaliation, the butcher allegedly used his butchering skills to resolve the matter with both his wife and her admirer. Fortunately, Ferdie escaped unscathed. When the news of the scandal hit the streets, Ann rescued Ferdie from further trauma by being sent to the pound.

Shortly after Ann's passing, my husband and I moved from Canada to the UK where Ferdie was still living with my father-in-law, John. Ferdie took to me immediately which, according to John, was not a surprise. Ferdie generally seemed to prefer women. Perhaps that preference came from his memories of the butcher, but his preference for me became evident on more than one occasion.

As Ferdie stood nearby, William reached out suddenly and grasped my upper arms in jest. Sensing a threat by William's abrupt movement, Ferdie gripped the bottom of William's trousers with his teeth and — growling menacingly — shook the trouser leg with a vengeance, causing a large tear. Given his relative size compared to William's height, it was obvious that Ferdie posed no real risk; but Ferdie's actions clearly indicated that he was my dog. He'd made it clear that he wasn't going to tolerate any abuse — real or perceived — against his new mistress.

While visiting John's home in Bromley, Kent, William and I camped overnight in the spare room, with two mattresses on the floor. At some point, William and Ferdie must have had a disagreement of some sort, leaving Ferdie bent on revenge. That evening, I went to bed with Ferdie cuddled up alongside me, but acting rather anxious. When William came into the room, Ferdie jumped over me to the wall-side of the mattress. He stared fearfully over my shoulder as William edged himself onto his mattress alongside. As William's feet reached the bottom of his bed, I heard a loud "*Ugh!*" At that, Ferdie snuggled even closer to me.

Have you guessed what happened? Yep. Earlier in the day, for reasons known only to him, Ferdie had gone into the room to sneak between the sheets of William's bed and had made a "deposit" into which William later pressed both feet. As I broke into fits of laughter, I could almost hear Ferdie "snicker" as he dashed over my shoulder and under the covers for protection. Obviously, William was not amused. The memory of that incident has brought a smile to our faces for many years (well, mine at least).

On one of our day trips out to the English countryside, we decided to visit Hever Castle and have a picnic lunch by a pond. Ferdie found this all very interesting, since trips out of the city were not something he had previously experienced.

As we sat quietly chatting and enjoying the scenery, Ferdie decided to take a dip in the pond. Problem is, Dachshunds have neither "keel" nor "rudder", so Ferdie began to roll precariously. As my dear father-in-law and I watched in horror, William was off to the rescue. Now, William was not a lover of beaches, the outdoors and especially not of swimming — let alone taking a most unwanted dip into a smelly pond. Fortunately, the pond was not very deep, so William had only to wade in, rescue the drowning mutt and deliver him back to shore.

Ferdie took the whole thing in his stride. He simply shook nonchalantly, cast William a dart-sharp look and settled in for lunch — leaving William smelly, dripping wet and uncomfortable for the remainder of the day. "Should have left the bloody thing drown," uttered William, much to the glee of my father-in-law whose shoulders were heaving up and down in a valiant attempt not to laugh out loud.

When we returned to Canada from England, Ferdie came with us. I swear, he barked all the way across the ocean. The barking didn't cease when we collected his crate at the airport. This was not a happy ex-pat.

Up to that time, Ferdie's outdoor experience had been limited to the fenced-in garden of an English cottage property so it wasn't surprising that he was mesmerized by the space in which he suddenly found himself: the thirty-acre property where my mother's home was located.

Given the size of the property, Mom had chosen to cut only a large grassy area around the house, leaving the remainder to grow for hay. Ferdie happily trotted around on the lawn, showing absolutely no interest in the hay-covered field.

One day at play time, we threw a ball that landed in the hay field, well beyond the trimmed grassy area. Ferdie went off in pursuit and jumped through the "fence" (really, just tall grass). This little head suddenly appeared, with Ferdie standing on his hind legs and looking very gopher-like with his front paws dangling in front of him. The stunned look on his face was hilarious. We could almost hear his little inner voice exclaiming, "What magic place is this?"

Ferdie adapted quickly to this newly discovered invisible fence thing.

With ever-increasing excitement, he started running wildly throughout the field — every now and then assuming his gopher-stance to check his bearings. This wide-open space is heaven, man!

Ferdie's next Canadian adventure was wading in a freshwater lake nearby. Unlike the pond at Hever Castle, he was able to saunter into the water from the shallow end and just go as far into the water as was comfortable. No rescues were necessary. It was here that Ferdie developed a passion for collecting rocks. He would dunk his head, collect a rock and bring it back to shore to make a stack. Ferdie would dunk-grab-and-deliver until he started to sputter from the intake of water, and we would have to make him — protesting — leave the lake.

When we moved into a house in Ottawa, my nephew, Garry, came for dinner and a short visit. As we were giving Garry the five-cent tour of the house, Ferdie was desperately trying to get Garry's attention. Garry was a gentle soul but, since we hadn't seen each other in a while, he was more interested in chatting with us than in responding to this persistent little dog. Regrettably, being ignored was something Ferdie simply would not tolerate — much to Garry's horror.

As we stood chatting, we noticed that Ferdie was strangely positioned with his back end pointing toward Garry's shoe. Ferdie would occasionally glance over his shoulder to check his position — much as a long-haul driver would back up an eighteen-wheeler. Suddenly, this horrible odour wafted upward. Yep. There sat a large wad of pipsqueak poo, perfectly centred on the front of Garry's Gucci shoe.

We're pretty sure Ferdie was smiling with satisfaction as he sauntered off with that expression of, Ignore me, eh? Well, take that! Perhaps Ferdie

---

## Do you know the difference between "purebred" and "pedigree"?

### SEE CLOSING NOTES

was giving solid form to the message voiced in *A Man for All Seasons*, "Good night. If we should bump into one another, recognize me."

Despite his size, Ferdie would take on any dog, anytime, anywhere. While I remained vigilant and protective, William observed that there was nothing to worry about. In his view, Ferdie would kill any size dog of any breed. He would choke them on the way down. Very soon, Ferdie's acceptance of an additional canine-companion would be tested when he was introduced to our beautiful Dayna.

# Dayna

Shortly after we returned from the UK with Ferdie, William and I spotted a "rehoming" ad of "military family posted to Europe looking to rehome loving female dog to good home." Given that William had served in the RAF and that both of us had lived and worked among  military families, we had tremendous empathy for the family's plight. We contacted the family and headed off for a meet-and-greet. Our only concern was whether Dayna would get along with Ferdie, our UK Dachshund with the big-time attitude of Make My Day.

As we pulled up to the military residence, there was a medium-sized black dog happily playing fetch with two children, with Mom and Dad waiting on the steps. Dayna had the facial features of an Irish Wolfhound

 and a body more akin to a Border Collie. Beautiful girl.

As far as the dogs were concerned, we need not have worried. Ferdie exited the car with his usual bravado. Dayna shot him a look of "Seriously, peanut?" She flopped to the ground and looked away with total disinterest … which

14

brought Ferdie to a shocked standstill. This is a match, we thought, with great relief.

We spent quite some time chatting with Mom and Dad about their posting, who we were, our history with dogs, how Dayna would be treated, where she would sleep. We also made sure to give lots of attention to Dayna.

By this time, we were longing to have Dayna become part of our family. Much to our relief, the parents decided that we could be trusted with their beloved family dog. Rather than cause the children any further stress by having us return another day, the family voted to have Dayna go home with us that very day. There were tears and hugs and promises of never forgetting the wonderful companion Dayna had been to each of them. We also promised to keep them apprised of everything Dayna.

Dayna adapted to us very well. Initially, any time she heard children's laughter or saw children playing, her ears would perk up. However, within a very short time, Dayna became William's shadow and followed him everywhere. Even when William headed to his vehicle, there was no way Dayna was going to stay behind. I soon adopted my mother's practice of several years before — if William didn't answer when I called, I would just call Dayna — knowing that, where she appeared, William would be there too.

To our amazement, Dayna was exceedingly well-trained, but her former family could only tell us, "She came that way." Apparently, they had adopted her from a shelter, so neither we nor they knew much about her past nor exactly how old she was. None of us could figure out why anyone would surrender such an amazing companion.

Dayna loved to play fetch with either a ball or a Frisbee. She enjoyed the Frisbee so much, she would play until her gums bled (if we let the game last that long!). In all the time Dayna blessed our lives, she missed that Frisbee only once — seriously, only once in an entire lifetime. One notable behaviour, whether ball or Frisbee, was that Dayna would return the toy directly into the middle of our lap. That always made us wonder whether her initial human companion might have had mobility issues and had played with her from a seated position.

Another strange phenomenon with Dayna was her reaction to fire.

Shortly after adopting Dayna, we moved from a house in the city to a multi-acre property in the country. The heating system was a combination oil and wood furnace and, in winter, we usually opted for the steadier heat of a wood fire. We soon discovered that it was not a good idea to allow Dayna into the basement when we went to fill the furnace. If we did, Dayna would stand between us and the open furnace door and do everything she could to prevent us from approaching the fire blazing inside. She would even give out a low warning growl, which was very unusual behaviour for her. Might she have been in a fire? Might her previous human companion have been injured or died in that fire? It would explain how this amazing wee girl had ended up in a shelter. We'll never know for sure, but we thank the Fates that Dayna became a part of our lives.

Shortly after we moved to the country, I began working from home. Unfortunately, I am one of those people who totally lose track of time when I am focusing on something. To her credit, Dayna wasn't having any of that. Most of the day, Dayna would lie quietly by my chair. BUT,

every day at precisely 4:00 pm, Dayna would rise, fetch her Frisbee and drop the Frisbee into my lap. She would then sit and wag her tail, her glimmering brown eyes shining with a look that clearly said, "Enough already. Time to play." And so we did.

A day came when we saw another dog in need of a good home. With Dayna and Ferdie in tow, off we went because (you guessed it) that other big dog would be rescued *IF* he were a right fit for our two precious fur-babies.

# Toby
## (aka Our Canadian Chicken Hound)

$A$h, Toby! All our fur babies are special, each in his or her own way, but Toby was just one of those dogs that stood above the rest — especially given his sad beginning.

Although we already had several fur-babies, our attention was drawn to the plea from a nearby shelter that desperately needed to rehome a very large dog. The dog's ginormous size was proving to be a barrier to adoption. In addition, the shelter didn't have a kennel sufficiently large for him, so he was beginning to go "cage crazy". Their concern was that confinement in a kennel of insufficient size might result in depression or even aggression — either of which had the potential to result in his being euthanized.

We just couldn't bear the thought of a healthy dog being put down. As for his size, we were living in a large old farmhouse on a large rural property, so size was not a major concern. We could make room for him. Our only requirement was that he had to get along with our existing duo — Dayna and Ferdie — or, at the very least, he had to give some indication that, with time and patience, he would be able to do so. Much like people, there should be no expectation that every dog will like every other dog at first sight.

Oh my. We could not have remotely imagined what was in store for us!

Upon arriving at the shelter, the attendant asked if we would like to go into the kennel area to see Toby. We declined on the basis that we knew we would not be able to resist all the other soulful eyes staring out at us. With a reluctant sigh, the attendant headed off.

A few moments later, the swinging door from the kennel area flew open with a bang. This huge mass of fur barrelled through, with the attendant trying desperately to hang onto the lead and doing a pretty good water-skiing impression across the tiled floor. She was holding on for dear life, the heels of both feet sliding along, with toes pointing upward and a look of total fear across her face. Wow. That was one big, powerful dog. We weren't sure whether to laugh or to take our leave.

Fortunately, there was nowhere for the pair of skiers to go beyond the reception area. William moved quickly to turn the lock on the front door to prevent any accidental escape. I snatched the leash from the now-terrified — but recovering — attendant and, strangely enough, Toby relaxed.

Once dog and people took a breath and a semblance of calm was restored, we were ready to hear Toby's story.

Toby was a mixed-breed, with the facial features and the height of an Irish Wolfhound, but with the tail and centre portion of his body more like that of a German Shepherd. He was absolutely gorgeous. Huge! But gorgeous.

Toby had been brought to the shelter by a family who'd claimed he was a stray. However, given his behaviour with the family and his initial

demeanour, shelter staff suspected that this might have been a covert surrender. Fact is, people don't always consider what might evolve out of that cute, cuddly mixed-breed puppy of unknown origin. It's a risk. But usually a rewarding one. Whatever the truth, these folks had made a wise decision to deliver Toby to a safe place rather than just abandoning him.

That was pretty much the extent of what was known about Toby's past — except for one other heart-wrenching fact.

Shelter staff told us that, prior to being put into a kennel, Toby had been given a bath, complete with anti-flea shampoo and a good brushing. During that exercise (which must have been quite the challenge), the staff could feel a hard surface around his neck. Initially, they thought it might be a scab of some sort. However, as they picked and tugged at it, they were horrified to find that it was actually a dog collar. A dog collar had grown into the skin around the neck and was covered in fur! The collar must have been placed on his neck when he was much smaller and never removed until that bath. As an observation in passing, Toby only ever grew a sort of "fuzz" in the area around his neck, but never any actual fur.

The past put temporarily to one side, it was time for the big meet-and-greet. The best place was outdoors, in a fenced area, to give all the dogs plenty of space to move freely. Normally, I am not an advocate of allowing dogs to meet "on lead"; however, for safety's sake, we kept Toby on a long lead to give him the feeling of freedom, while keeping our two precious babies safe.

***

Ferdie, our Dachshund, ambled over with great bravado, looked up, and up, and up, and gave out a menacing growl (not) and a threatening bark to which Toby's reaction was, "Seriously, magpie?" while looking somewhat surprised, but without even the remotest sign of aggression toward Ferdie's challenge.

Dayna's reaction to Toby was much more congenial. She moved closer, wagged her tail, looked up. Yep. Even she had to look up. She and Toby did the nose-to-nose greeting followed by the Lemme  Check Out Your Butt routine. It was a match.

Fortunately, we had travelled in two vehicles and Toby came home with us that day, with a pre-arranged stop at the vet en route for a quick check. We wanted to make sure there were no health issues that might affect our other animals and that might require Toby to be kept in isolation. That examination revealed a serious ear infection that would soon be diagnosed as so severe, part of the inner ear had to be surgically removed.

A covert sign that appeared over time to suggest what this lovely creature might have endured was that, throughout his life, Toby would react with a snarl if any man wearing heavy leather gloves came anywhere near him. Obviously, there was an untold story that would remain a mystery, and it wasn't a good story.

Toby's transition to living with us was by no means a cakewalk, but time, training and patience (LOTS of patience) would reward us with one of the most amazing dogs ever.

The very first thing Toby did when he entered our house was lift his leg on the dining room table. So, challenge number one: house-train an almost adult dog. (Sigh.) I say "adult" because, although the shelter staff figured Toby was about two years old, there were numerous other indicators of his being much younger than that. To my utter dismay, we soon discovered that Toby was still in the Chew-Everything Phase, not the least of which were shoes (but only *my* shoes) and only one from each pair. I simply renamed myself the One-Shoe Wonder.

Bottom line: large does not equal mature.

Despite some early challenges, Toby proved to be a great student and, within a very short time, he mastered not only the house-training but also his own personal signal of Time To Go: usually a stand on all fours, a tail wag, and what can only be described as a smile.

Ah, the tail. Toby was a happy boy, with a constantly wagging tail that swept across everything in its path, so the coffee tables, side tables and some low-lying surfaces were temporarily removed. Over time, we could leave food on the few remaining low-level surfaces and he wouldn't touch anything; but, if he turned around, that tail would just wipe the surface clean — glasses, plates, food and all.

We always thought that Toby didn't take any interest in the other furniture, but we couldn't figure out why the love seats were so full of fur. The mystery was solved when, unbeknown to Toby, we looked in the window and saw him sprawled across one of the love seats, his head hanging over the armrest at one end and his hind legs at the other. Yep. He was that long.

Toby became part of our family when William and I were going through our back-to-the-earth phase and enjoying life on a large rural property complete with chickens, honeybees and two geese that we had inherited (but those are other stories). This was the perfect environment for a dog as large as Toby, with lots of space to run and play with our beloved Dayna.

With the house organized to accommodate our newly acquired Toby, I continued to travel to a job in Ottawa about a hundred kilometres away. One day while I was away, William noticed that Toby was unusually quiet. He called out to Toby but, receiving no response, he went off in search. William knew the exits were all secure, so Toby had to be somewhere in the house. Where could a dog that large be hiding?

As he toured the main floor area, William could hear a muffled *uhhhh uhhhh* that he followed to the mud room at the back of the house. There he found Toby, standing on his hind legs, towering a full head-height above our neighbour, with a front paw on each of her shoulders. With our neighbour securely pinned to the wall, Toby's tongue was slurping up across her face from left to right as though her face were an ice-cream cone.

After a commanding "Toby, off," Toby returned all four paws to the floor, whereupon our neighbour (who had a major fear of dogs) grabbed for the door and scurried off to her vehicle.

When I returned home, William recounted the incident, beginning with an exasperated, "You won't believe what YOUR dog did today!" Seriously. I couldn't stop laughing. All I could muster was, "Well done, Toby! That's my boy. Treat?"

The reality was that this particular neighbour had a habit of walking in without knocking, even though we weren't close friends, so I had little sympathy for her self-inflicted experience. On the positive side, from that day forward, our neighbour never, ever walked into our house unannounced. In fact, she would drive into the yard, park close to the mud room door, beep the car horn, roll the car window down and chat to us before leaving the vehicle. I can only reiterate, "Well done, Toby!"

For the most part, Toby and Dayna stayed close to home, but Toby had inherited the sight-predominant characteristic of his Irish Wolfhound genes and, on at least one occasion, he followed a bird and couldn't find his way home. Fortunately, Toby had very distinctive features, was well-known in our close-knit neighbourhood and, thankfully, was retrieved within the hour. Our gracious neighbour had lured Toby into his dark, unlit garage — not knowing that Toby was desperately afraid of the dark. Toby's experience must have made an impression, because he never again went roaming.

With his happy, gentle demeanour, combined with some professional obedience training, we had yet another perfect canine in our fur-bearing team. This sweet boy could carry an egg without crushing it or a small turtle without injuring it — even a squirrel that he dropped unharmed. The garden snakes I really didn't care about, but even those he would only carry and not crush.

One day, I spotted Toby coming toward me from the barn with a chicken in his mouth. My first thought was — horror of horrors — he had killed a chicken. As he got closer, I said, "Toby, put it down," with the intention of taking the dead chicken away from him so he wouldn't feel rewarded for his efforts. Ah, me of little faith!

Toby put the chicken down, whereupon the chicken shook itself off and simply walked away, no worse for the experience. When we checked the fencing around the coop, we found that several chickens had edged their way underneath the fencing and were roaming around, with Toby retrieving and returning them to their proper place. Toby's interest in the chickens proved to be friendly, bloodless and downright protective.

Because of the wildlife roaming freely around us (bears, wolves, foxes, raccoons — you name it), we let the chickens roam during the day but, at dusk, we would put them into the safety of a chicken coop. Given Toby's protective instinct, all we had to say was "Toby. Chickens," and he would round them up with great precision. He also had precise counting skills.

I would anticipate that most people have not had the experience of trying to count free-range chickens but … they are in constant motion. William and I would try to count the thirty-six layers, then one would move and we'd have to start over again. We soon learned to put our faith in Toby with "Toby. Chicken missing." Toby would put his head into the chicken coop and, if any were missing, he would go off in search and bring them back — totally unscathed. Conversely, if all the chickens were accounted for, Toby would simply lie down at the door and refuse to budge. We have absolutely no idea how he managed all of this, but we were duly impressed.

When the day came for us to unburden ourselves of the chickens, one of the local egg farmers came by to collect them. As the farmer chased around the yard in a futile effort to catch them, we suggested that he simply put the crates down, wait for Toby to round up the chickens and close the doors once they were inside. The farmer's look of disbelief quickly melted into total awe. "Wow, with the size of my free-range flock, I could really use a dog like that. How much do you want for him?" But there was no way we were ever going to part with our "Canadian Chicken Hound", no matter what the monetary offer.

Toby was also amazingly sensitive to human needs.

When my mom visited, she enjoyed working outdoors — feeding the chickens, raking grass or whatever — and Toby would follow her around. In later years when Mom started to suffer from a heart condition, she still enjoyed short walks outside, but she was unsteady unless holding onto an arm or walking stick. Amazingly, Toby would position himself alongside her so she could place her hand on his back for balance and the two of them would have a saunter around the yard. Lovely sight!

Bringing this gentle giant into our home was the best decision ever. He was truly *mine*: protective, loving, and constantly present. Toby holds a very special place in my heart. Forever loved. Forever missed.

---

**Abuse and Cruelty = an offence under Canada's Criminal Code.**

SEE CLOSING NOTES

# Lady

As volunteer animal cruelty agents for the SPCA, William and I visited local shelters quite often. On one of those visits, I spotted this gorgeous white dog with tufts of golden-brown fur and the most piercing green  eyes I had not seen since my childhood friend, Digger. Her stare was hypnotizing — and just anchored me in place.

Not much was known about her. She was a stray with no tags, implants or anything else to identify her, yet she was obviously well-fed, in good health, house-trained and well-mannered. It seemed strange that no frantic calls had been received from her humans in search of her; however, her minimum release/pre-adoption period was not yet up, so there was still hope. The only concern was that she was cage-pacing,. which is never a good sign for a dog that might have a potentially lengthy shelter stay.

My heart went out to her. I couldn't resist that spellbinding stare. Fortunately, given our affiliation with the shelter, William and I were already pre-screened for both foster and adoption. The shelter staff assured me that she was "dog friendly" and I already knew that our three would be fine. If any problems arose with our cats, I felt confident that those little beasts would have the wherewithal to band together and sort her out. All factors considered, I offered to take her home for the weekend. It seemed only fair to give such a beauty a break from the confinement and offer her a chance to exercise with some four-legged companions.

As soon as I pulled up to our house and William saw the dog, the first words out of his mouth were "Not another one!" I assured him that Lady would be with us "just for the weekend." William rolled his eyes in total defeat.

The meet-and-greet with Ferdie, Dayna and Toby went off without a hitch and we settled in with four dogs. Temporarily. BUT. You guessed it. The Fates were at play. The "weekend" extended to the end of her shelter release period, whereupon Lady became a permanent part of the team.

Our snow-white beauty had been given a shelter-name that we didn't much like. We couldn't decide on a suitable alternate; however, the light bulb went on when we witnessed her eating habits. No matter how much

food we put in front of her, she would eat until every morsel was devoured. That caused William to say, "Listen, my lady, you had best get a grip here. There's lots more where that came from." The name stuck and "she" became "Lady".

Lady's eating habit was curious since we offered her plenty of food. First stop in solving the eating mystery was a visit to the vet to confirm that there was no health-related issue. The vet concluded that, although Lady had done well for herself, she might have been on the streets for a while. As a result, Lady had developed the attitude of Better Eat Up since she didn't know when or if there would be a next meal.

We struck upon a possible solution. I sat with Lady — a dish, a bucket of water and a bag of dog food within reach. When she emptied the bowl of food and had a drink, I would wait a while to allow enough time for her brain to tell her tummy she wasn't hungry. Then I would refill the bowl — always careful (as the vet had cautioned) not to overfeed her to the point of making her ill. After a few refills, Lady flopped onto the floor and stared at the bowl, without touching it. Message received. Never again did she gorge.

Caution: NEVER do this without advice from a vet. With some dogs, it's just their nature and you could end up with a very sick pet — or worse, a dead one.

Although Lady's obsession with dog food subsided, she never lost her taste for people-food. We had to keep a close eye that she wouldn't do a grab-and-run if given a chance. That talent might well be the way she managed to keep fed on the streets, but it was most annoying within the confines of the house. Nonetheless, there are times when one just forgets, or is distracted. Lady didn't miss any opportunity.

One day, I was working in my office while William was in the back yard with Lady and Toby, while focusing on preparing food for a BBQ. My office window looked out over the back yard and, when I suddenly heard William shouting, I looked up. Whatever could be wrong? Did one of the dogs get through the fencing? I was just about to go out to help when all the commotion became obvious. There was Lady with a juicy steak dangling out of her mouth, darting around the yard in circles with William in hot pursuit. Within seconds, William had cornered Lady and, as he reached for the steak to determine if it would still be edible, Lady swallowed the steak. Whole. Don't worry. Lady was just fine (it was a small steak), but it took William a while to get over the defeat.

Lady was a sweet girl who was captivated by William and dearly wanted to take Dayna's place in William's world. After a few warning snarls, Lady got the message and was smart enough to keep her distance. When the day came that Dayna crossed the rainbow bridge, Lady didn't waste any time wedging her way into William's heart and personal space.

Peace reigned in our household while Lady became fast friends with Toby. The two were inseparable, cuddling together and sighing in mutual contentment.

One of the area foxes was bewitched by Lady. At every opportunity, Mr. Fox would "sing" when he saw Lady, trying his best to get her attention. We never did figure out what the allure was, but it happened day after day. Sometimes, Mr. Fox would sit and croon from a position on the hillside, staring down in love or lust. Lady would escape by jumping into a wooden half-barrel outside the back door with her back to the hill.

A fox's bark is plaintive and unmistakable. It echoes over long distances, so there was no doubt that Lady could clearly hear his lovelorn call. However, Lady was enamoured with Toby and she would not be enticed by any of Mr. Fox's attempts at courtship. Faithful hounds to the end ... and beyond.

Despite her rebuke of Mr. Fox's advances, Lady and Toby were quite happy to befriend Ms. Skunk. Although William and I maintained a safe distance — just in case! — Lady, Toby and Ms. Skunk would traipse happily along the bottom of the hillside in what we assume was a deep philosophical conversation, totally without incident. However, a problem arose when we made our annual pilgrimage to the seaside and, on our very first day at the cottage, a skunk appeared. Obviously, this was not the same skunk. With great excitement, our friendly pair darted off to say hello. It did not end well. Lady took a direct hit. After a hefty salt-water bath followed by a fresh-water rinse, Lady was confined to the outer deck until the aroma wore off.

Lady and Toby remained inseparable. When Toby crossed the rainbow bridge, we thought we might lose Lady. The bond between them had grown very strong. Lady stopped eating. She stopped interacting with us, other than the occasional tail wag. She sported a soulful look with those beautiful green eyes. The vet couldn't find anything physically wrong with her and concluded that she was mourning, to which I responded, "But she's a dog." To which the vet responded "And your point is?"

Enter Gretzky … and Lady recovered, giving us the joy of her company for several more years. Lady and Gretzky were a good match for each other, but the bond between them never reached the depth that she'd had with Toby.

# Gretzky

Gretzky was an English Springer Spaniel ("pedigree", not simply "pure-bred"). Gretzky's lineage was sufficiently formidable for even the Royal Family to be impressed.

Gretzky and his siblings were pre-purchased before they were born. However, shortly after taking up residence  with his new family, Gretzky developed some mobility issues. As per the terms and conditions of the purchase agreement that is standard practice for *reputable* breeders, Gretzky was returned.

Once back in the breeder's care, veterinary tests determined that Gretzky had been born with a condition that the vet coined "crooked leg syndrome". Since this had never happened in any previous litters, the breeder was both perplexed and devastated.

After considerable research, the breeder discovered that this is a rare — but not uncommon — condition that appears without rhyme nor reason in any and all dog breeds. Expensive surgery followed. Although Gretzky would have a life-long disability, the breeder was of the view that at least Gretzky had a fighting chance for a good life. Lengthy and intensive therapy followed, including swimming to exercise the limbs without inflicting stress or strain.

Sometimes the Fates intervene just when they are most needed.

At six months of age, with surgery and initial therapy complete, Gretzky was ready to be rehomed. About the same time, we were at our wits' end over what to do to entice our dog, Lady, out of her depression over the loss of our mutually beloved Toby.

Coincidentally, the breeder also operated the boarding kennel we used so we were a known entity. Given that Gretzky needed a relatively low activity environment and given that Lady was now older, with little desire to romp and play, the breeder considered ours to be a suitable home. It was just a matter of, did they like each other? Thankfully, it was a match.

Gretzky was a sweet boy, full of personality. He would get up on the couch and drape one front leg over the arm, looking ever so regal.

Gretzky appeared intensely interested in people-conversations. He would make and maintain eye contact and listen attentively, hanging on to every word. His poise earned him the name of Mr. G. (Far more elegant than being named after a mere hockey player.)

Gretzky was by far the most relaxed pooch we had ever encountered. Nothing fazed him — not noise, not people, not strange encounters. He had a calm, composed demeanour that gave off the vibe, "Relax, man. Come on over and have another toke, eh?" which, admittedly, we often voiced on his behalf.

Although he was well-healed from his surgeries, Gretzky still required regular, but moderate, exercise — especially swimming — to provide light exercise for his limbs. We were fortunate to find an aqua therapy facility for dogs nearby and arranged regular appointments. The therapists were amazing and, at each visit, Gretzky was so anxious to get into the pool, he soon became a special favourite of the therapy team.

In an effort to delay mainstream drugs for as long as possible, Gretzky also underwent acupuncture offered by our local vet. The treatments served him well, with his full cooperation. He would stand patiently while the needles were inserted and then quite happily parade around the room looking very much like a canine pincushion. He would then stand quietly as the needles were removed and he was rewarded with one of his favourite treats.

Gretzky's vet visits for monitoring proved both interesting and amusing — especially on first-time visits for x-rays by a new staff member. The usual remark was, "We'll just give him a mild sedative to keep him calm." *Sigh.* If there was one dog that did *not* need to have drug-induced calm, it was Gretzky. My comeback was always, "Just give him a try first and if he needs medicating, you can do it then." The vet tech would lift Gretzky onto the x-ray table whereupon, with an exasperated look of, "Ah, man. This again?" he would lie down and roll over onto his back, well-versed in this familiar routine.

Although Gretzky's on-the-hoof mobility remained limited, even he could not curb the temptation of chasing wild rabbits. Regrettably, he mustered enough energy and short-distance speed to actually catch one or two, and eat them, creating some other rather disgusting results that I choose not to share.

When it came to caring for his own personal comfort, Gretzky was no dummy. If his limbs started to bother him, he would just roll over onto his back to relieve the pressure — a habit that one day proved to his advantage.

When Gretzky accompanied us to an outdoor fundraiser for a dog rescue group, most of the doggie games were beyond Gretzky's physical ability — except for one. When the Dead Ant contest was announced, I noticed that Gretzky was showing signs of "relaxing". We hurried into the ring and at the shout of "Dead ant", Gretzky wisely chose that very moment to roll over onto his back with all four legs pointing straight

upward. Yep. Gretzky won over all fourteen competitors and was awarded a bag of treats. And a ribbon.

Mr. Personality was also very vocal. Not only did he "chat", he also acquired a love of singing. As Shania Twain's hit "Honey, I'm Home" was playing, Gretzky began "singing" along to the tune. It was right out of the blue, without any training or prompting. Ever after, whether the recording was playing or whether one of us just belted out a few bars, Gretzky would start to sing along. Fascinating.

When William retired, we moved to Prince Edward Island onto a property within walking distance of the Northumberland Strait. This afforded Gretzky ready access to what he loved most: swimming on a daily basis for a good part of the year.

In no time at all, Gretzky became well-known among beach goers for his Olympic swimming skills. If the tide was just right, he would swim way out into the Northumberland Strait to a sandbar where he would then stop for a short rest and a quick sniff of the shells and seaweed. Some days, the sandbars were too far under water, but Gretzky would just keep on swimming toward the opposite shore, en route to Nova Scotia and New Brunswick. That brought screams of concern from the children on shore who were fearful that he would drown. Fortunately, Gretzky seemed to have an internal gauge of his own limits and a sixth sense of when he was "half way". That's just as well because there was no way I could swim as well as he — nor as far — in order to rescue him.

Much to the delight of beach goers, Gretzky would occasionally swim back to shore in the company of the solitary seal that resided nearby. It was quite a sight. The seal and Gretzky swam a respectable distance apart, keeping an eye on each other. One could almost hear the seal's thoughts of "What are you? And why are you all the way out here in the Strait?" Once Gretzky got to shallower waters, the seal would turn away with a splash, but not before casting one last curious look over his shoulder at the strange, furry, swimming thing he had encountered.

When Gretzky was on his way down the beach stairs, he was totally focused on getting to the water and oblivious to all the activity around him.

On one occasion, there were two children on the beach who went into a major panic attack when they saw our sweet boy bounding down the stairs. They started to scream at the top of their voices, with plastic buckets and shovels flailing in their hands and stamping their feet into the sand. Two adults, whom I assume were the parents, sat in beach chairs a few feet away, pretty much mirroring their objectionable children. All four were lucky because, had they displayed this inappropriate behaviour with a dog less placid than Gretzky, there might well have been serious consequences. And, of course, it would have been deemed the dog's fault.

In any event, as Gretzky reached the bottom of the beach stairs, he glanced briefly to his left with a look of, "Eh. What's your problem?" Without stopping for even a nanosecond, Gretzky plodded merrily into the water for his daily swim, leaving the children (and the parents) staring in shocked silence, hands, pails and shovels frozen in mid-air. Ah. That's my boy.

Most encounters were much more amiable.

One of the cottagers enjoyed kayaking at high tide and, as he was paddling along, Gretzky nonchalantly swam by. The kayaker's stunned look said it all, with perhaps a bit of concern of what Gretzky might do, but Gretzky's interest was in swimming, not hitching a ride. He simply shot a side glance at the kayaker and kept going merrily along his way.

As Gretzky got older, he was no longer able to get down the beach stairs so we started going to one of the beaches in Victoria-by-the-Sea where he could walk into the water from ground level. Even then, Gretzky's swimming prowess drew admiration from beach goers. He would often make it out and around the buoys that serve as warning signs for incoming fishing vessels, quite a considerable distance away.

Not all of Gretzky's escapades were necessarily droll. Sociable as he was, one day he chose to swim toward several people involved in an array of waters sports: canoes, Sea-Doos and water-boards. Even from a distance, I could see that they were so absorbed in their various sports, they would be unlikely to spot Gretzky's little brown head bobbing in the water.

As my panic level increased and my calls of "Come" to Gretzky went unheeded, I stormed into the water hoping to distract him from all the dangerous water activity. Par for the course, as soon as I was foolish enough to start swimming in hot pursuit, Gretzky turned around and placidly swam toward me. My first reaction was relief. My second was annoyance since, in my pocket, was the key fob for my new vehicle, a key fob that never worked again.

The day came when Gretzky would spend only a few minutes in the water and then return to the beach, lie down and stare out longingly at the ocean. His loss of passion for the water was a warning sign. Fortunately, the thing he liked best after swimming was to cuddle up beside me, with his head in my lap. We did a lot of that and, throughout it all, his happy personality never wavered.

When Gretzky became part of our family at six months old, we were told that he would need on-going pain medication and that his life projection would be about four years. The Fates were kind. His need for pain meds didn't kick in until his interest in swimming stopped almost twelve years later. Cuddled beside me in his favourite spot on the couch, Gretzky crossed the rainbow bridge at the tender age of 13-plus, just five months shy of his fourteenth birthday. Love conquers all.

Gretzky and Lady.

## Do you know how to identify a "reputable" breeder?

### SEE CLOSING NOTES

# Wirm

W irm was likely a "purebred" Yorkshire Terrier: the product of two parents who were both of that breed. However, since no record was provided of his lineage, he would not have been recognized as "pedigree".

Off the top, you might ask, Why was this dog named Wirm?

Well, the name his previous humans had given him was Thomas but he didn't seem to know that name and certainly didn't respond to it. He was a dog that wouldn't sit or stand still. Whether he was being held in your arms or sitting (well, sort of) in your lap, he would wriggle. He was in constant motion, the ultimate ADHD dog. Because he wriggled like an earthworm, I jokingly said that I would call him "Worm". My sister said, "You can't call a dog Worm." To which I responded, "Fine. I'll spell it with an *i*." Hence, the name Wirm, to which he did learn to respond.

Regrettably, Wirm's history is not unique.

Wirm was surrendered to the shelter by his owners who claimed he was too dangerous to have around children. The poor little guy had rotting teeth, scanty fur, bare patches, itchy skin that he constantly scratched, poor eyesight, ear mites. The list goes on. Simply put, Wirm was an elder dog in need of care, not abandonment. Given his age, his physical condition and his somewhat nasty attitude, Wirm's chances for adoption were rock-bottom.

The last thing William and I needed was another dog, especially one with so many issues; however, given his age and physical condition, we figured he was entitled to a few years — or even a few months — of a caring, comfortable environment.

Despite our love of dogs and animals in general, Wirm taxed us to the limit with his health issues and his behaviour. We were fortunate to have a vet who went above and beyond the call of duty to do extra research on Wirm's various conditions and to keep the rising vet bills manageable.

One of the more baffling of Wirm's issues was his skin condition. The medical tests were inconclusive and, despite our vet's ongoing efforts, she remained puzzled as to the underlying cause.

Considering the extreme state of Wirm's fur and skin, it was reasonable to assume that the problem had existed for quite some time. In order to shed some light on the possible cause, a member of the shelter staff was asked to contact the previous owners. It would have saved time, trouble and expense to know if any diagnoses had ever been rendered

and what treatments might have been suggested. Regrettably, the response from the previous owners was essentially "We surrendered him. He's your problem now," and hung up the phone. We were back to square one.

As is always the case, desperate situations require desperate measures. Our vet went the extra mile and took the liberty of contacting a reality-TV vet who had a TV show at the time. Thankfully, he was very gracious and suggested that the root problem might be food. Based on his experience, he suggested that Wirm might be allergic to the rice in the high-priced lamb-and-rice that was his diet at the time. The TV vet recommended a diet of boiled fish and potatoes, with a vitamin supplement. Within a few short weeks, Wirm's itching stopped and the bald spots began to grow back. It took substantial time and effort, but Wirm soon began to look like a normal Yorkie.

With Wirm's skin issue resolved, it was time to have the worst of his rotting teeth removed and then to focus on his behavioural issues.

Wirm was very protective of his food. He also hated white shoes and would attack them with a vengeance. These behaviours suggested that he might have been teased to get a reaction. We were only ever able to surmise but perhaps Wirm's response might initially have been considered amusing; however, the behaviour would have become a serious problem once grandchildren began to appear — with all of the blame falling to the dog.

Wirm hated men, initially including William. Since I was the one who had rescued Wirm from the shelter, William deemed Wirm to be my problem and kept his distance from this unruly little dog.

On one occasion, poor William got a bit too close to me for Wirm's comfort and Wirm grabbed William's nose with a vengeance. Picture it: William standing in the middle of the floor with this little Yorkie hanging from his nose, blood dripping everywhere and Wirm wriggling as much and as hard as he could. William was yelling "Get him off," but the scene was just too funny for me to keep a straight face.

Eventually, Wirm let go of William's nose, jumped back up beside me and growled his dissatisfaction as William went off to tend to his wounds. I don't think William ever forgave Wirm for that incident; but neither did William come close to me when Wirm was nearby.

A somewhat amusing sidebar on this occurrence is that, just a few weeks later, a video of a Yorkie displaying a similar behaviour on one of the reality TV shows actually won his owners ten thousand dollars. I observed, had we filmed the incident of Wirm and the nose attack, we might have been that much richer. William was not amused.

Wirm's life with us was not all horror story.

Wirm was not averse to chasing things bigger than he was, so he wasn't deterred when he spotted the mare up in the paddock. He was off like a shot. Up and under the fence he darted, chasing the mare in circles. All of a sudden, it seemed to dawn on the mare that it was rather silly to run away from something smaller than her entire nose. The mare suddenly turned and started to chase Wirm instead. Wirm quickly circled back, ran as fast as his little legs could take him and dashed under the fence to safety. He then turned around, wagging his wee tail as if to say "Gotcha."

Unfortunately, Wirm's chasing habit also took him in pursuit of a skunk — a skunk that turned on him in retaliation. Unfortunately, in my effort to save him, I was also caught in the spray. Such is life with a dog.

Wirm really was a character, with lots of personality, objectionable though it was at times. He was OCD when it came to squeaky toys. When we got tired of listening to the constant squeak of a rubber toy he had, we would put it out of reach to give our ears a rest. Wirm would stand for hours just staring up at it, completely transfixed. We learned very quickly that all toys had to be hard rubber or soft plush with no noise makers inside to risk disturbing our peaceful existence.

When we went on vacation, my aunt Weenie would house/pet-sit for us. By that time, Wirm was much calmer, had a well-established routine and was showing signs of having a fun personality. When we returned home, my aunt recounted that she had thrown her woollen slipper at him for doing something he shouldn't. Even if she had tried her hardest, the woollen slipper couldn't have done any damage. I gave Wirm a cuddle and said, "Did mean Auntie Weenie beat you?" Whereupon he lifted one paw as if to say, "It was this one she hurt." Thing is, each time he showed how hurt he was, he lifted a different paw.

With time, a good diet, his health restored, furry companions and a safe environment, Wirm lived quite a happy life for several more years. He was cherished. We often think of him and all his trials and tribulations, satisfied that we had created at least some good memories for him.

---

### Children & Animals.

#### SEE CLOSING NOTES

# Astra
## (aka June)

Whenever Lady crossed the rainbow bridge, we were concerned about leaving Gretzky on his own while we were at work. We didn't want to risk any loneliness that might lead to separation anxiety.

Gretzky's breeder told us that, in keeping with the purchase agreements for all her puppies, an adult male Springer Spaniel had recently been returned by a couple going through a separation/divorce. Although we've never been attached to a particular breed, the fact that this return needed rehoming was of interest, so off we went for a meet-and-greet. Regrettably, the meeting of these two alpha-males was not an immediate match and, yep, Gretzky could be alpha when he so chose. No disability was going to stop him from standing his ground. Given our respective work schedules at the time, it would not have been fair to either dog to take on the time-consuming challenge of getting them to accept each other.

As we turned to leave, the breeder said, "Wait just a moment. I have a little girl that might suit you. She's lovely but I know from experience that she does not have the personality to be a successful show dog. As a pedigree, she might be difficult to place. But she would likely do quite well as a pet."

Before we had time to say yes or no to a puppy, the breeder had already placed little black-and-white "June" into William's arms. William was still suffering from the loss of his faithful Lady and, when "June" cuddled into his neck and stared up at him with her sparkling brown eyes, it was a done deal. Gretzky wasn't quite as enthralled at the idea of this wee furry thing jumping all over him, but his low, guttural growl was more one of annoyance than anything serious. It was a match.

William soon decided to highlight his RAF connection by renaming his new puppy Astra, after the insignia of the RAF, in plenty of time for her pedigree documents to be submitted with this preferred name.

As a couple, we had always adopted older dogs, so it came as a surprise to learn that Astra was actually William's very first puppy. Ever! This created some concern on my part. I had been there done that in the somewhat distant past and I remembered how much time was involved. Nonetheless, the undertaking proved to be more than amusing to watch.

The first order of the day was to establish a routine for William's little girl. Part of that was taking Astra outdoors for frequent visits. Most puppy owners will relate to the fact that no matter how many trips are made to the grand outdoors, the puppy will invariably pee as soon as it comes back in. Punishment for this behaviour is both futile and counterproductive and actually slows down the desired outcome. Success is simply a matter of time, patience (lots of it), persistence and repetition. Fortunately, our TV/relaxation area had tiled floors that made for easy cleaning. Armed with a roll of paper towel, a mop and a pail of water always at the ready, William got lots of bending exercise during those first few weeks of tending to his first puppy.

We've always crate-trained our dogs, carefully limiting the confinement to short periods and eventually just leaving the door open to allow the crate to become the dog's personal, safe space. Then, if the dog has to travel or, the Fates forbid, a medical stay at the vet is needed, the dog's stress level is considerably reduced. Our good intentions notwithstanding, the first few nights were challenging.

After being placed in her crate at bedtime, Astra began whining and howling, even though Gretzky was in full view in his open-doored crate alongside her. Soft-hearted William desperately wanted to rescue Astra and take her to cuddle with him, but that couldn't happen, at least not until Astra was house-trained.

I don't know who drew my greatest empathy: suffering William, wailing Astra or sweet Gretzky who had to endure all the uproar. In any event, we decided to put an old-fashioned ticking clock in under Astra's blanket. Soon she was quiet. That ticking clock trick works wonderfully well, but in today's world, finding a ticking clock is difficult enough, let alone one that is safe, without any biteable bits.

Astra adapted quickly to her night routine, but she was quick to recognize the signs that bedtime and crating were about to happen. One evening, William's attempts to get Astra into her crate were met with Astra's dashing this way and that in a valiant effort to avoid capture, giving William some unwanted exercise. Gretzky sat quietly, observing these antics until he obviously decided this silliness had to end. Off the couch he slid and walked casually into the open crate, followed by Astra. That gave William the chance he needed to close the crate door just as Gretzky exited and returned to his comfy couch with that look of "There, Dad. That's the way it's done." This became a regular routine even after both Gretzky and Astra slept in open-door crates.

Obviously, Astra couldn't spend all day during puppy-period without a toilet-break. Fortunately, William's place of work was only seven minutes' drive from our house. So, the puppy-possessed William went home during his morning break, his lunch break and

his afternoon break until Astra was sufficiently well-versed in the concept of Pee Outdoors Only.

Soon it was time for Astra to get some basic training. Despite having had several dogs over the years, it's easy to forget what to do during the initial training stage. A refresher was in order.

As true dog people know, obedience training is much more for the human than for the dog. The dog will do what it is taught once it becomes accustomed to the verbal commands or physical gestures that are incorporated — combined, of course, with tempting treats. Unfortunately, it can be difficult to find a trainer who believes in Enticement with Treats and Praise rather than resorting to a quick fix using a device to force the behaviour.

One particularly disturbing experience was with a trainer who recommended a prong collar. In my view, this type of collar (among others) is never a good choice, regardless of the type of dog. My response to this suggestion was, "A prong collar on a Springer Spaniel? Are you out of your mind?" The trainer's explanation was that William would be more focused on the prongs potentially hurting Astra and that awareness would

help William to loosen up on the lead. As we made a very quick exit from the training facility, with the trainer's eyes widening in disbelief, my response was, "Fine. If William is the problem, then put the prong collar on William."

Astra soon completed an array of different training with more-suitable trainers. One habit that William found annoying was that Astra would jump up in greeting when he arrived home — largely because he would call out, "Where's my girl?" causing Astra to race toward him. In a discussion with one of the trainers, William explained that he had no problem with this when

he was wearing casual clothes, but not when he was wearing his business suit. The trainer smiled knowingly and asked, "So how long do you think it will take Astra to distinguish between the two types of clothing?" The light bulb went on. Astra never did learn that distinction.

For basic agility training, William and I attended the classes together. At one point, William was visibly disappointed that Astra would do some of the exercises for me and not for him. After taunting him for a while with "Gosh, I guess she just likes me better," I came clean. I had yummy dog treats tucked into the end of my mitten, so of course, she was anxious to perform for me. Oldest trick in the book.

Astra formed an attachment to one particular toy that she acquired

as I was going through a bag of plush toys. She fixed her stare on this one particular black-and-white "dog" that was the spitting image of her. Given the puppy's rather delicate construction, I was a bit reluctant to give it to her, but couldn't resist those big, brown eyes. It proved to be the right decision.

Astra remained enamoured with this plush puppy, kept it on her day bed, slept with it and carried it around as her constant companion. We even had to take it from her when she headed outdoors. Although her frequent licking caused the puppy to become threadbare, Astra never tore it or damaged it in any way. It was her baby.

Although Astra quite enjoyed watching Gretzky swimming to his heart's content, she never got any more than her feet wet, despite being a so-called "water dog". She would cast a look of "Honestly, Gretzky, I don't get the hype over all this wet stuff."

As the breeder had foreseen, Astra was the perfect dog for William. Neither of them liked swimming nor the bugs that are a part of the great outdoors. She preferred to snuggle comfortably onto William's lap and luxuriate in being stroked while William read. It was a match made in heaven.

## Do you know what to look for in a dog trainer?

### SEE CLOSING NOTES

# Cats We Have Served

Diana Lariviere

# Michael Edward
## (aka Mikey)

For a few years, it just wasn't practical for me to have any pets. I also held the view that animals should have access to the great outdoors, rather than being confined to an apartment. I convinced myself that if I did get an animal, it would have to be one that for some reason could not roam freely outdoors. The Fates were obviously listening.

As I walked by the pet store in a nearby mall, I spotted these little kittens in the window, romping and having a great time. I couldn't resist going in. Just to take a look. The shop clerk told me that one of the male kittens, white with blue eyes, had been returned after just a few days. Apparently, the kitten would not respond to the buyer's child. He surmised that the kitten might be deaf, and nobody wants a defective pet. Right?

Well, there it was. This kitten needed a home and, in keeping with my self-imposed condition, he was not a good candidate for the outdoors. He wouldn't hear any of the things that might pose a danger to him. Kismet!

Armed with a new litterbox, cat food, toys and other stuff, kitty and I went "home". Little did I know that this particular fur-baby was the start of a lifelong rescue trend.

The day after his adoption, I shared the story of my new deaf cat with my boss, a kind-hearted gentleman with whom I had an amazing working relationship. After a bit of teasing, I said, "You know. I just might name him after you since you never listen to me either." And there it was. Deaf kitty was named "Michael Edward", "Mikey" for short.

Mikey grew into quite a large beast and a force to be reckoned with. With me, he was cuddly and loving, but if he disliked someone, he could be quite creative finding ways to express his displeasure. Over time, Mikey learned a sort of sign language. If he didn't like the command, I gave him, such as "get off the furniture," he would stand up, turn around and lie down again — facing the opposite direction. One cannot do what one is told if one cannot receive the instruction. Smart cat.

Mikey developed a taste for alcohol and became a beer connoisseur. — something we discovered when we spent time at my sister Linda's tourist establishment. Despite all efforts, Mikey would slip into the bar unnoticed, knock over the bottles and slurp up the dregs. If we didn't watch closely, patrons who knew his passion would set out tiny saucers of beer in response to his meowing. It certainly wasn't the healthiest of habits — for a cat. It just was what it was and he was never allowed to consume any more than a slurp or two.

Mikey (neutered) was also in love with my niece's cat, Min-Min (spayed). Soulfully, Min-Min didn't share the same feeling for Mikey. She would turn her back on him as he rolled and purred on the opposite side of the porch screen.

When my sister Linda came for a visit, Mikey adapted to her routine. When she was about to come in each evening, he would jump on top of the refrigerator near the door. As Linda entered, Mikey would reach, grasp her hair with his paw, pull the hair into his mouth and shake his captured "mouse" with all the force he could muster. Thankfully, Linda loved him and cheerfully endured this rather rough greeting day after day.

Mikey wasn't quite so charming to my nephew, perhaps feeling somewhat skittish because of Ronnie's gruff-sounding voice and his 6'4" height. When Ronnie came in wearing a Stetson-style hat that added to his height, the terrified Mikey jumped straight up into the air from the trunk on which he had been sitting, and peeing liberally during his flight.

A few years after Mikey became part of my life, my employment took me to Nova Scotia. At one point, I travelled a lot. With no family or close friends nearby (at least none that liked cats), I had to find a safe place for Mikey to stay while I was on the road. I was fortunate to find a boarding kennel for cats called the Pussy Pause Motel in Peggy's Cove/Indian Harbour. I will leave it to your imagination as to what went through my mind when I first saw the name of this establishment, but it was heaven-sent.

The ad read something along the lines of "Quiet private suites with sunny outdoor decks overlooking St. Margaret's Bay." The owner, Barbara Corbin, ran one of THE poshest catteries I have ever seen — until then or since. Barbara was very attentive to her guests' health and comfort and would readily administer a cuddle when needed. Mikey loved staying there, to the point that he was seldom in a hurry to leave when I arrived to pick him up. Barbara often had to nip into his "suite" or out onto his private deck where he lay luxuriating in the sunshine and overlooking the ocean. He would meow in protest as she put him into his travel kennel. He was one pampered cat.

Mikey also became a trendy air traveller — especially after I relocated to Goose Bay, Labrador, for work.

On one occasion, Halifax airport was fogged in and the plane was rerouted through Toronto and back to Halifax. (Yep. Made sense to me too.) With the short reboarding time in Toronto and the fact that luggage is rarely transferred as quickly as passengers, I had serious concerns that cargo-travelling Mikey might be left behind, out on the cold tarmac at Toronto airport. I headed up the jet walk but then stood one foot in the plane and one out, refusing to  board until Mikey was found. My actions certainly did not make me flavour of the month with the crew but, much to my relief, Mikey was boarded onto the same plane as I.

As anticipated, my luggage didn't arrive until the following day, but Mikey arrived safe. The Fates must have approved of my taking such a strong stand on Mikey's behalf because the only seat available on the plane by the time all this kerfuffle ended was in first class. My reward was a lovely brunch, complete with sparkling wine. Thank you, Mikey!

Mikey was a significant part of my life long before I met my husband. Suffice it to say that Mikey and William never really bonded. Their relationship was akin to It's The Cat or Me, but my sentiments were with the cat.

Mikey wasn't about to give up his status as my number one roommate. I would wake up to the sound of snarling (by the cat) and grunting (by my husband) as each tugged at opposite corners of the quilt. Mikey usually won.

When William and I were preparing to move to the UK, William continued packing while I went out on an errand. When I got home, I found William carrying a curtain rod in one hand to "defend" himself. Apparently, Mikey had positioned himself at the landing on the stairs and, every time William went up or down, Mikey would lash out and attack his leg. Mikey was obviously expressing his opinion, How Dare That Man Disrupt Our Household!

Mikey travelled to the UK and back to Canada with us. It's a wonder he didn't have his own frequent traveller card. When we settled into a house on a large rural property about a hundred kilometres outside Ottawa, Mikey was able to safely go outside a bit more, although his favourite spot was by the patio door, soaking up the sun.

As our cat community grew to a total of six (along with four dogs), Mikey remained "king" as the only male cat among them.

Mikey lived to the ripe old age of sixteen. In all that time, he never grew any closer to William than he had on their first encounter. Mikey was unique among felines and definitely a cat with personality.

**Did you know: a significant number of blue-eyed white cats are born deaf.**

# Fickle & Fancy

When the local shelter issued a plea for help during an upper respiratory outbreak in the cat section, William and I answered the call. We chose two mirror-image calico kittens: one primarily black with orange and white patches and the other primarily white with orange and black patches.

Both kittens had shelter-issued names that we have long since forgotten; however, their spirit-animal names soon became obvious based on their personalities and behaviour.

The primarily black calico was tiny and demure, with an elegant "presence", so William named her "Fancy". Fancy became a constant presence on William's shoulder when he sat in his La-Z-Boy to read or

watch TV. She would sometimes curl herself around his neck, creating the image of a fur collar.

Conversely, the primarily white, or blonde, calico would match every inappropriate and politically incorrect blonde-bimbo joke on the face of the earth. She

55

was curious, impulsive and constantly getting herself into trouble. William named her "Fickle".

Soon after bringing our two fur bundles home, it was obvious that the primarily black one, Fancy, had contracted the upper respiratory illness that had spread in the shelter. This was worrying; however, a vet visit had already been arranged for a general health check-up, as well as to schedule any required shots and a spay date. All went well. Within a few days of receiving the vet-prescribed medication, she showed significant improvement. She was also quite vocal when we placed her in solitary confinement to protect our other animals from infection, so we knew she was improving.

Although Fancy recovered from her early respiratory infection, her health remained somewhat fragile. In springtime, both William and Fancy suffered from hay fever. Despite their suffering, it was rather amusing to watch them. William would sneeze, and pretty much in unison, the shoulder-perched Fancy would follow up with a sneeze of her own. No doubt they both found us (well, me) rather callous. But funny is funny!

Fickle would occasionally cuddle, but only if it were on a day that suited her. Unfortunately, Fickle was an escape artist, with a tendency to roam. She worked really hard at using up all of her nine lives. Fickle once disappeared for over three weeks and then returned to us. From a distance, she looked relatively unscathed; however, when William gathered her into his arms, it was clear that she had suffered a hip injury. With veterinary oversight, she recovered quickly.

Fickle was one really observant feline. On one of those blustery winter nights with gale winds whirling snow around the house — essentially, "no night out for man nor beast" — William and I were relaxing amidst our usual entourage of dogs and cats. As sometimes happened, Fickle had deigned to sit on William's lap that evening. She suddenly began to stare intently upwards, toward the skylight. Naturally, our eyes were drawn upward as well.

At first, all we could see was the snow, glistening along the window-pane of the skylight. Then we saw what Fickle had spotted. At the top edge of the window, a mouse appeared, unsuccessful in his efforts to gain access to the warmth of our sitting room. Mr. Mouse then began skidding along the slick edge of the window in a futile effort to regain his footing. Slowly but surely, with all four legs outstretched — much like a cartoon character — he slid along the angled windowpane from the top all the way to the bottom … and disappeared. Fickle was adamant that she was going to get that mouse and spent the rest of the evening running up and down the stairs, across the floor, up and down from the indoor window ledges, trying to figure out how to get "up" to the window and the now-long-gone mouse.

Fickle and Fancy remain in our hearts. Every time we think of them, we recall the joy they brought to our lives.

# Suishi

As to how Suishi came by her name, it's just one of those things that happens accidentally. On the day we decided to invite her into our home, we had gone out for an order of our favourite sushi. I jokingly said, "Let's call her Suishi, but with an *i* so as not to confuse her with the fish." The name stuck.

Suishi was a stray that was dropped off at the local shelter. She was an older cat, with all the signs of having had kittens fairly recently, but there were no kittens to be found. Given her mild demeanour, it was clear that Suishi was not feral and that she must have been someone's house cat. One possibility is that, once the kittens were born, Suishi might have been abandoned in favour of one of her kittens. Beyond that, her history is unknown.

Regrettably, Suishi was diagnosed with mastitis, an infection of the mammary gland that can cause fever, loss of appetite and vomiting. If left untreated, the result can be serious infection, extreme pain and even death. Among the causes is breast milk accumulating but not being expressed.

As often happens, the Fates intervened. At the same time, a litter of kittens, totally unrelated to Suishi, had been found and also brought to the shelter. The shelter staff was hopeful, subject to any treatment Suishi might need, she might accept and feed the litter. It was a match made in heaven. Suishi was an affectionate motherly cat, more than happy to share her milk and affection with this unrelated mess of kittens.

Once the kittens were old enough to wean, Suishi's fate had to be decided. It did not appear to be good.

Suishi was obviously an older cat — although exactly what age would only have been a guess. Given her age and the fact that many kittens and younger cats were available for adoption, Suishi's chances of finding a forever home were minimal. Euthanasia was on the horizon.

When William and I heard about Suishi's plight, combined with her background story of having saved an entire litter of kittens, we just couldn't resist adopting her.

After being spayed, vaccinated and given a thorough vet examination, Suishi joined our clan of five cats and four dogs. She was a friendly sort and fit in without incident. She wasn't much into hunting, but she enjoyed meandering about in the outdoors. Her most favourite things were being cuddled, lying in the sunshine in front of the patio door (along with all the rest of the fur-crew) and finding a cozy, comfortable bed. Her motto became "Relax, man. No need to rush, eh?" After all she'd been through, she deserved that luxury of a happy retirement.

# Patches

Patches was one of several kittens produced by a stray cat (aka Mamma Kitty). The kittens were on the verge of turning feral by the time my mom discovered them under her back porch. Despite the challenge, my persistent mother eventually got the "kindle" into her guest trailer where there was plenty of space for them to safely run about. The ongoing care and nurturing of the kittens was left to Mamma Kitty. To her advantage, the resort-style accommodation provided Mamma Kitty with private space to dine alone, with an above-floor perch high enough to have a rest from her brood.

The origins of Mamma Kitty are unknown. My mom's telephone calls to surrounding neighbours in her small rural area and the posting of a notice at the community mailbox didn't unearth an owner. Given Mamma Kitty's friendly demeanour, she definitely had lived among humans. Best guess is that she was dumped by a passer-by — a common and cruel practice by people who mistakenly believe that cats can fend for themselves.

In any case, this story ends well. My mom adopted Mamma Kitty, including having her spayed and vaccinated as soon as medically possible. All the kittens were adopted out to close family members.

Once the kittens were old enough to leave Mamma Kitty, William and I were among the first to visit. This gave us first choice, albeit a difficult one. The kittens were each so different — not only in their colours, but also in the texture of their fur, their budding personalities, et cetera.

Ultimately, our choice was a spunky little girl who wasn't entirely sure whether she should be friendly. She hissed and spat and wriggled, clearly demonstrating her displeasure at being groped and handled by these strange beings. This was definitely the right fit for us: outspoken and independent.

Patches had long, silky, angora-type fur in patches of black and white, and a face that would melt your heart. One particularly interesting feature was that her primarily white back legs had tiny, symmetrical black patches that made her look as though she were wearing mukluks as she walked away. Really cute! Not surprisingly, we named her Patches.

In record time, Patches settled in with our fur-team of three cats and four dogs. As soon as she was old enough, Patches (like Mamma Kitty) was spayed and vaccinated.

Patches's favourite get-away-from-it-all spot was the downstairs bathroom sink. She was just the right size to coil into a circle, with her head tucked toward the drain.

During a visit with us, my mom got the fright of her life. As was her habit from living in the country, Mom would often walk around the house in the dark, carrying a flashlight. Late one night, William and I heard a blood-curdling scream that sent us tearing down the stairs. There we found my mom hanging onto the bathroom sink, breathing heavily. Apparently, as Mom had reached across the sink to turn on the water tap, her hand had skimmed across a very warm, furry body. Yep, Patches. All rolled up in her favourite spot. Patches couldn't figure out what the fuss was all about. She stretched, yawned, curled up into her usual ball and went right back to sleep, totally oblivious to all the commotion.

Patches appreciated both her canine and feline companions. She would nuzzle up to the dogs for a mutual sniff or settle in with one of the other cats or on whichever of our laps might be free.

Patches also enjoyed her time outdoors, touring the barn and the chicken coup for treasures that she would proudly deliver to the back door: Late of this parish, but not eaten. After all, why eat a mouse when one could enjoy gourmet cat food?

When work caused us to relocate to Toronto, we knew our fur-babies would no longer be able to enjoy the freedom of the outdoors. Although we had a six-sided cat run installed so the cats would be able to spend time outdoors, our efforts were futile. Patches, in particular, proved to be an escape artist, thereby jeopardizing her safety within the city limits. By this time, another cat had joined our family. In collusion with Patches, they made it very clear that they were not — and did not want to be — city cats.

---

**Do you know how many kittens can potentially be produced in one year by one UNspayed female?**

SEE CLOSING NOTES

# Topper

$T$opper was among a litter of five kittens that were found abandoned at the local county dump. When she came to us, her eyes were still closed and she had to be bottle fed at regular intervals.

This kitty soon developed a love of climbing, including all the way up to my shoulder. Hence the name Topper.

Never having known her mother, Topper figured I must be it, so she developed the habit of clinging to my pantleg and just hanging there while I carried on my daily activities. As Topper's self-confidence increased, she was not averse to trying this with visitors, many of whom were bare-legged. In anticipation of potential consequences, peroxide and Band-Aids were kept close by.

Topper's fondness for climbing continued into cat-hood. She would find the highest point in any room and suddenly descend upon unsuspecting passers-by who would shriek in surprise as she landed on their head or shoulder.

Like most cats, Topper enjoyed the warmth of a small space and soon discovered that she was tiny enough to fit between Toby's back legs (our Irish Wolfhound/Shepherd mix).

One evening as we sat quietly with our fur-family strewn about the room, Topper fell into a deep slumber within the warmth of Toby's legs.

Since she was still very much a kitten, she began to knead (unintentionally and without malice) into Toby's tender parts. The sudden pain caused the napping Toby to suddenly jump about three feet off the floor, startling all of us. Except for their look of surprise, both were unscathed and, within the hour, had reassumed the same positions — both falling into another comfortable slumber.

When we moved to Toronto, we discovered that Topper, along with her close buddy, Patches, were truly not city cats. For anyone who has lived in Toronto — or any large city, for that matter — there is a constant *hum* from the traffic, the airplanes, air conditioners, the subway, whatever.

Topper's reaction to the change in environment was totally different from that of her soulmate. Instead of trying to escape to just about anywhere as Patches was doing, Topper would flatten herself on the ground or the floor. She would lie there for hours, all four paws spread-eagled, refusing to move.

Rather than see the cats suffer, our niece (Line) and her husband (Mark) agreed to take them to live with them in the country by a lake (tough life!). Within seconds of opening their travel crates, both Patches and Topper found a comfy spot and fell into the best sleep they'd had in weeks. They were "home".

A few weeks later, we went back to visit Line and Mark — in large part to see how our precious kitties were doing. The reaction of Patches and Topper was identical. They were both downright indignant. They ignored us completely, cuddled up beside Line and threw us a disgusted stare. So much for loyalty, eh?

---

**Do you know that it's illegal in Canada to abandon an animal?**

**SEE CLOSING NOTES**

# Cruel "fun"

One evening, at a time when we had four dogs and six cats, we suddenly noticed that there was not one cat to be seen and things were just a wee bit too quiet. That sent me off in search of the six little demons.

In the living room, I found all six cats crouched in a circle. This was odd because a few of them didn't get along all that well. Suddenly, I saw movement. There, in the centre of the circle, was a tiny mouse. Each time the mouse would try to escape, a cat paw would come up and smack it back into the centre. No doubt Mr. Mouse would eventually have met his demise; however, much to the dismay of all six cats, play time was terminated. I returned the mouse to the great outdoors.

# Line Decarie's Cats
# & A Couple of Dogs, too
## Line Decarie

# Two Tommies and a Prince

I have wonderful memories of all the fur-babies that have been part of my life. Although I grieve deeply when they pass over the rainbow bridge, I can't imagine living without one.

My first vague animal memories are of a small, black, mixed-breed dog named Prince.

He was my dad's pride and joy before I appeared, to usurp that role. Although many fur-babies would follow him, I consider sweet and gentle Prince to be my very first dog. He never objected to having his "hair" combed or wearing a scarf or even wearing rosary beads — much to my mom's dismay if the priest chose that very moment to visit.

Grandpa obviously thought that I should have a companion of my own and surprised me with a kitten that I named Tommy. After all, he was a *tom*cat.

Much like Prince, Tommy (later renamed Old Tommy) would let me dress him up in doll clothes and push him around in a doll carriage. Tommy became my soulmate. As I grew up, he would sense my moods and just seemed to have a sixth sense of when to cuddle and purr in an effort to distract me.

My mom loved my pets as much as

she loved me and insisted that they be treated with kindness and respect. No infraction was excused on the basis of "She's only little." This is a lesson I carried through to my adulthood and later impressed upon my own child.

In the past, spay/neuter was not widely practised, so Tommy would wander. One day, he disappeared, and despite all efforts, Tommy was nowhere to be found. We feared the worst and I was heart broken.

In an effort to ease my grief, my beloved Grandpa arrived one day with a little black kitten. This wee critter had a dot of white on his neck,

fur that was long and silky, and beautiful yellow eyes. Not surprisingly, we chose to call him "Little Tommy". He loved to be pampered by being brushed in bed, held in my arms, and covered with a blanket.

About six months after his disappearance, and much to our surprise and relief, our original Tommy suddenly reappeared — fat and happy. As often happens with cats, Tommy had found a happy place to vacation for a while. He settled back in as though he had never been away.

Now we had two cats named Tommy, so we opted to rename them Old Tommy and Little Tommy, respectively, to distinguish one from the other when we were talking about them.

# Min-Min

The time came for me to leave home to attend school, find employment and begin my own journey. I had never been away from my family before. I felt lost and alone.

Given the love of animals instilled in me by my grandpa and my mom and dad, I couldn't resist strolling through the nearby pet store. There I found the solution to my loneliness when I spotted a teensy black and white kitten that reminded me of another that had passed over the rainbow bridge. There was something about her that I just couldn't resist, so Min-Min came home with me that day, complete with all the food and accessories she would need.

Min-Min and I bonded within minutes. Except for those hours when I had no choice but to leave her while I was at school or work, we were inseparable.

I always felt guilty about leaving her alone, so I would leave a dish of special treats sitting in the middle of the table for her to enjoy. These treats looked a lot like "people" candy, but I never saw a need to put a note on them marked Cat Only. I should have known better. One day when I was visited by Great Aunt Betty, who was somewhat sight impaired. I went to make her a cup of tea and when I came back, Auntie said, "I hope you don't mind. I had one of the candies on the table. They're very tasty, but a bit on the salty side." I nonchalantly removed the dish from the table, not having the heart to tell her she had just eaten a cat treat.

Min-Min became quite an experienced traveller. I didn't have a vehicle, so my only mode of transport was the passenger bus which, at that time, did not allow animals. After a bit of training, Min-Min learned she had to be very quiet when I put her into my travel bag.

City travel didn't pose much of a problem, but our two-hour weekend bus trips to visit my family posed a challenge. I would do my best to sit at the very back of the bus, well out of view and of earshot of the driver. After an hour or so, Min-Min would naturally get restless, pop her head up and give out a low meow in protest. This could have been disastrous, but because she was so cute, none of the passengers ever snitched on us.

Throughout the time we lived in the city, Min-Min was quite happy as an indoor cat and didn't come in contact with others of her kind. One exception was Mikey, a large white male cat that occasionally visited my family at the same time we did. Mikey was enamoured of Min-Min but the feeling was not mutual, so we kept the screen door closed between them. Poor doting Mikey would rub up against the screen door, curl his neck inward and purr or meow loudly to get her attention. Alas, Min-Min's only response was to turn her back to him and gaze out at the scenery.

# Blacky

The day came, when together with my husband, Mark, Min-Min and I moved into a large, lakeside house in the country and Min-Min was finally able to enjoy the outdoors in safety.

A skinny black cat with one tiny white patch on his neck and big, sad, yellow eyes appeared at our door. He won our hearts with one look. We named him Blacky.

Given his sweet and gentle demeanour, Blacky might have been left behind by summer cottagers — perhaps accidentally, perhaps intentionally. Regrettably, there's a mistaken belief among the ill-informed that cats can fend for themselves.

After a vet visit to ensure he had no health issues, followed by neutering and the required vaccinations, Blacky was introduced to Min-Min and that was the start of a beautiful relationship. Other than that first vet visit and mandatory vaccines, Blacky was never sick a day in his long life.

With good food, love, attention and time, Blacky grew into a gorgeous tomcat with silky black fur, bright yellow eyes and an actual mane that circled his neck like that of a lion's. His only interests were love, affection and food. He hated the cold and left any hunting expeditions to the various female cats that joined our clan along the way. That said, Blacky was very gentlemanly. He always deferred to the female cats — to the point of taking his meal only after they had all eaten. Blacky definitely fit the description we gave him of "Gentle Giant".

## Abandonment & cruelty = Offence under Canada's Criminal Code.

### SEE CLOSING NOTES

# Rambo

Word must have gone out to all the stray and abandoned cats in the neighbourhood because the next cat to appear was a mangy-looking male with a nail lodged in his back. Obviously, we couldn't ignore his needs, so it was off to the vet to have the nail removed.

According to neighbours, this people-friendly cat had been in the area for quite some time and had become known as Rambo. We can only surmise that the name was linked to the movie character of that name who is depicted as tough, reckless and aggressive. Actually, that was a pretty accurate description of this cat.

Although people had occasionally fed Rambo, no one had taken him in. We figured that it was time for Rambo to have a *furever* home. Once he recovered from his nail injury, Rambo was given a general health check, neutered and vaccinated.

When Rambo was introduced to Min-Min and our first stray-rescue, Blacky, the introduction did not go well. Moreover, despite our greatest

---

## Do you know what to do if you suspect animal abuse or abandonment?

### SEE CLOSING NOTES

---

efforts, the relationship did not improve over time. Nonetheless, we were committed to ensuring that Rambo had a permanent home — including love, healthcare, food and his fair share of attention. We simply adapted by ensuring that all three cats were never in the same place at the same time. The Fates smiled upon us when they brought Rambo into our lives and we had no regrets about the extra effort it took to keep all three cats safe and happy.

# Sassy

Every true animal lover knows that love and loss are unavoidable parts of inviting an animal into our lives. We love each and every one of them for completely different reasons. When the time comes for a well-loved pet to cross the rainbow bridge, we mourn that loss. Sometimes, the pain in our hearts is manageable. Other times, circumstances make the loss more difficult to endure.

My beloved Min-Min had come into my life when I had recently lost a parent, when I was setting out on my own for the first time and when I was feeling lost and alone.

Although my husband, Mark, and I still had several other feline companions that we adored, I felt I simply couldn't take another cat into my life. Having witnessed the deep grief I was feeling, Mark refused to consider taking in a new pet. Fortunately, my aunt, with whom I share a strong love of animals, saw differently.

My aunt appeared at our door with this tiny black-and-white kitten. She asked if we could "foster" until she was able to find a permanent home for it. As if! That nasty lady (I love her, dearly!) knew full well that Mark and I wouldn't be able to resist falling in love with this little bundle of fur.

Sassy didn't take long to settle in and make her mark. The name "Sassy" was instantly obvious.

From the start, Sassy made it clear that she would not stand patiently in line. She ate first. She demanded attention when she decided it was time, no matter which other animal might be in our lap ahead of her. She quite literally confiscated my son's childhood foam chair for her own use. The Fates forbid if any other cat dare use it. Despite being tiny all her life, Sassy would never back away from a taunt. She remained a force to be reckoned with.

Unlike our gentle giant, Blacky, that preferred to sit quietly in the sunshine, Sassy was a fierce hunter, returning with an array of jack rabbits, snakes, frogs and mice that she carefully laid out at our doorstep.

Sassy also had a keen sense of which human to endear herself to: obviously, the most resistant one. She was successful in her endeavours and very soon became Mark's favourite kitty.

# Bandit

**B**andit got his name because of a white section under his mouth that looked like a bandana, so hence, the name "Bandit".

My vet of many years was well aware of our affinity for animals in dire need. Not surprisingly, when a stray grey and white cat was brought into his clinic, he called to ask if we would help as the cat might have to be euthanized.

By this time, it had been two years since our very first rescue, Blacky, had passed over the rainbow bridge. Even when a fur-baby is lost to us after many long and happy years, I find the deep sense of loss nearly unbearable. My husband, Mark, is the same.

We were more than a bit reluctant to agree, but our amazing vet said he would vaccinate, neuter and tend to the overall care of this "moggie" (a term that my British Uncle uses for a nondescript cat).

When Bandit came to live with us, he was afraid of anything and everything. To give him time to adjust, we gave Bandit free run of the upper level of the house — complete with food, water and litterbox. We also placed a baby-gate at the bottom of the stairs. This allowed Bandit to roam freely without being harassed by the rest of our fur-family while being able to stare out at what would eventually become his human and animal companions.

Several weeks later, Bandit suddenly appeared, jumped the gate, sauntered into the living room, sniffed the terrified dogs and casually made himself comfortable in his forever home.

Our dogs, Chopin and Chase, overcame their initial apprehensions to happily accept Bandit into the fold. Much to our surprise, Chase and Bandit soon formed a close bond. Given Chase's size, one might assume that Chase would be the defender. Not so. Bandit became Chase's protector. Bandit might have appeared small, but — perhaps as a carryover from his days on the street —he would not suffer any intruders.

When our neighbour's gentle German Shepherd, Taz, came into our yard to visit his buddy Chase, Bandit would run Taz — or any other dog or animal, for that matter — out of our yard and back within its own boundaries. The scene of a relatively small cat forcing a dog many times its size out of the yard has amused many an onlooker. Of ongoing concern was the fact that Bandit didn't always come away from those escapades totally unscathed. Many a bottle of disinfectant and a bandage have been applied to his minor wounds, but it all happened in seconds so there was little hope of stopping him.

Despite this aggressive attitude toward non-resident animals, Bandit had a totally different attitude toward humans. He loved people, loved to be cuddled and stroked, preferred to sleep upside down and enjoyed all his creature comforts.

Bandit had been with us for ten years when he crossed the rainbow bridge and we have no idea how many years he walked the earth before that. The pain of loss is fresh, but our love for Bandit will remain forever.

# Sophie

Our feline rescue, Bandit, must have been quite satisfied with his new digs and our treatment of him because, one day, he introduced us to a cat of many colours, a calico.

It was late afternoon when I saw Bandit over at the neighbours and thought he was acting strangely. He didn't seem to want to come to me so I walked over to investigate. There was Bandit, actually meowing his concern and drawing my attention to this little, multi-coloured kitten. The name that immediately came to mind just seemed to suit the tiny little ball of fluff. Welcome Sophie.

At Bandit's insistence, I carried Sophie back to the house, tidied her up, fed her and then canvassed the neighbours to see if she belonged to anyone. With her origins undetermined and no claims to her, Sophie became part of our clan. That decision was followed by a visit to the vet to check her health, vaccinations and, of course, the all-important spay to prevent unwanted kittens. It was then we discovered she had already been spayed.

Sophie is gentle and loving with humans and generally tolerated Bandit, her rescuer. Nonetheless, the two were known to get into an occasional scrap that required intervention. Sophie may be teensie tiny, but she has the roar of a tiger and an independent nature that would be admired by even the staunchest feminist.

As much as we love her, we refer to Sophie as our "devil child". A common characteristic of female cats is that they will kill anything within reach and Sophie is no exception. Regrettably, she kills things we would prefer she let live. In some cases, we also wonder how she managed it. We can only surmise that the delivery of these choice kills are her warped sign of affection.

Sophie causes us the greatest embarrassment when we take her into the vet for a checkup or to update her vaccinations. At last count, it took THREE vet techs to restrain her for even the simplest of examinations. In an effort to save us from embarrassment and to minimize her stress level, we searched out a mobile vet in the hope that Sophie would be calmer being examined in her home environment. I swear she reads the writing on the van or she smells the vet coming. The appointment went almost as badly as those in the past.

Much to our amusement, Sophie has a schedule by which we can set our clocks. She sleeps all night, deigns to rise around 10:30 am to eat, then returns to her slumbers until 3:00 pm. Depending on the weather, Sophie then chooses between hunting or trying to sit on my keyboard while I desperately try to work, whatever suits her fancy on the day. If Sophie chooses the keyboard, it's often best for me to just take a break and hope I have no incoming Zoom calls. Still, I suppose, it's much better than a human inadvertently appearing naked before the camera.

# The Kitty Clan

There were several other cats that came into our care — not because of abandonment, but because it was in their best interest. We became the "drop box" (in a very positive sense) for a few cats that needed a safe and loving home.

Among these were Patches and Topper, two cats that could not abide the vibrations within a large city when my uncle's work required him to relocate. Their story is for my aunt to tell.

When my beloved grandmother died, the care of her cat, Minew, was assumed by my mother. Sadly, Mom passed away just over a year later. Minew came into our care.

# Little Prince

When I was about twelve and our original dog named Prince had crossed the rainbow bridge, my parents introduced another, small, mixed-breed dog into our lives. This pup had a very similar look to our original Prince, so we chose to call him Little Prince. We went everywhere together: in my parents' vehicle, in my dad's truck and, much to everyone's surprise, flying.

At the time, my dad owned a small two-person plane that could be landed on floats, skis or wheels, depending on the time of year. Unlike most dogs, Little Prince had no fear of the roar of the plane. He would quite happily jump up and dance around in anticipation of the upcoming flight. Once seated on my lap in the plane, Little Prince would quietly enjoy the scenery.

# Chopin

During my apartment dwelling days, a cat was a more-suitable choice for companionship. My Min-Min didn't need regular walkies and was quite happy with a clean litterbox. However, when my husband Mark and I moved into a house of our own, all those childhood memories of my canine friends rose to the surface. Now that I had the space and access to the great outdoors, I dearly wanted a dog of my own. I also wanted my son to experience the camaraderie that I had enjoyed as a child. Unfortunately, Mark was more of a cat person and did not relish the idea of a dog being added to our cat harem.

As luck would have it, my aunt and I decided to visit our home town and, while there, we went shopping in the mall — the mall that just happened to have a pet shop. Yes. There, in full view, was a litter of puppies ready to be rehomed. The shop owner assured me that these mix-breed puppies would be on the small side, so memories of our two beloved dogs named Prince immediately sprang to mind.

Although I would like to have taken all of them home with me, common sense prevailed, and my attention was drawn to this one particular pup. I think it was his *yap* that seemed to say, "Take me. Take me." Or perhaps it was the fact that he seemed to be moving toward me. In any case, I was in love.

My aunt was well aware of Mark's position on dogs, but her attitude was, "If you want a dog, you shall have a dog." We left the store with the puppy that would be named Chopin, along with a few other necessities. The problem now was how to convince Mark that having a dog was a good idea.

As we drove homeward, we concocted a brilliant story. Or so we thought.

We both knew, that despite his refusal to have a dog, Mark was a soft touch when it came to animals — especially when cruel or objectionable treatment was involved.

As soon as we got out of the car, Mark spotted the dog and said, "Oh, yeah. What have you got now?"

Our mutually agreed upon story was that we had been driving home and there, alongside the road, was a man waving this little puppy in his hand. When we stopped to ask what was happening, we saw that the man had a box of puppies. He told us that he was trying to get rid of the puppies and, if there were any left at the end of the day, he was going to drown the remaining ones. So, of course, we had to save at least one.

Mark looked from one of us to the other, obviously sceptical of our story; but it was credible enough that the puppy was welcomed into the house.

Our cover story worked well for a few months — until the day that I wasn't home. Mark received a call from the pet store to remind us that Chopin was due for his booster shots. Busted!

By time, Mark was hooked on the cuddly, furry bundle that looked up at him with big brown eyes and followed him everywhere. It didn't hurt that Chopin liked all the things that Mark loved to do: the water, swimming and even balancing on a doggie-size

surfboard that Mark would tow behind him through the water.

Nothing deterred our brave wee boy, not even the sound of the ATV. Chopin so enjoyed his joy-riding that Mark built a special seat for him — complete with a seat belt for safety — so that Chopin could go everywhere with him. Now THAT is true love. So much for the guy who didn't want a dog.

# Chase

Chase was another accidental acquisition.

Totally out of the blue, my son, Eric, turned up with a friend carrying a cardboard box with a jet-black puppy in it. Apparently, another friend had a female dog that — foolishly — had not been spayed, the result of

 which was that she produced an unwanted litter. My son had figured, *What was one more fur-baby in our household?*

We certainly didn't want a large dog, so my first question was about the breed or the mix. My son replied, "Dobie and Lab." I froze at the thought of having a Doberman, even if it was a mix.

My immediate reaction was to send the puppy back to the person who had foolishly neglected to spay the female. Eric answered simply, "OK. I'll do that tomorrow," knowing full well that I would start to cuddle the little bundle of black fur. Chase never left and, despite his large size, grew into the most gentle, loving dog on the planet. (At least as far as I was concerned.)

I'm certain that Chase thought he was a person. He loved food — a bit too much — being caressed and he relished his various creature comforts. He confiscated a part of the couch that, thankfully, was large enough to accommodate his eventual size.

In addition to swimming, Chase would tread slowly and silently through the water and *fish*. Now and again, he actually caught one, but would let it go in surprise when it started to wriggle.

Largely due to my friend Joan, Chase acquired a huge selection of toys that we stored in a basket. Chase would react to my announcement that "Auntie Joan is here," by going to his basket, searching through, selecting the most recent toy she had brought him and greeting Joan with it at the door.

Chase was adept at hide-and-seek. I would say "I'm going to hide," and Chase would wait patiently until Mark would give him the command "Find her." Chase would then dash around the house in a mad search. Sometimes, I would jump out from my hiding place, with a loud "Boo" that caused him to react with a sudden jump, with all four paws lifting simultaneously off the floor.

Given his size, Chase needed lots of exercise — a fact that helped both Mark and I to become healthier.

The one thing that Chase absolutely detested was travelling in a vehicle — and that was a concern since I am a chronic shopper ... But I digress. In all likelihood, Chase connected the vehicle with going to the vet even though we brought him for rides to visit other friends or just to go to another trail to do a walk. I always felt bad that he never experienced the sheer joy you see in so many dogs with their heads sticking gleefully out the car window.

The most precious thing Chase ever gave me was my life.

When Chase was about nine years old, I accidentally fell from our deck — a distance of about eight feet — and was severely injured. I was all alone at the time, with no neighbours within shouting distance and my husband not expected back from hunting for at least a week. Were it not for Chase barking frantically and continuously on the deck above me, I likely would have lost consciousness. Thanks to Chase's persistence, I managed to slowly drag myself into the house to call 9-1-1 and then a nearby neighbour. Chase never left my side as I waited for help to arrive. Afterwards, he remained vigilant during my long, painful recovery. Thanks to this beautiful spirit that I had almost refused to keep, I lived to see another day.

Sadly, despite our greatest efforts, we were unable to save Chase's life. Just one year later, Chase was diagnosed with bone cancer. Although he survived the removal of the cancerous leg and was well on his way to adapting to being a tripod, the cancer spread.

When all options were exhausted, Chase crossed the rainbow bridge. I envision him running through the meadow on all four legs and completely free of pain.

Even though I know there is probably another fur-baby out there in need of my love and care, my heart aches far too deeply to invite another dog into our home. Maybe … Someday. But there will never be another Chase.

---

## Do you know that animals can donate blood to help other animals?

### SEE CLOSING NOTES

# Rural Tidings & Animal Tails
## (yes "tails" not "tales")

# The "Littlest Horse"

## Abby Sawyer

# Tiz Brave Heart
## (aka Willie)

I've always loved horses, spending every free moment of my childhood learning about them, consuming any horse-themed book with a furor, and begging for any time with them I could get. I spent years learning through books and the school of hard knocks, getting as much experience as I could before taking the plunge into horse ownership. Finally, when I turned seventeen, the most marvellous colt walked into my life.

In the summer of 2010, I spotted an ad out of Barnstead, New Hampshire, USA, for a registered American Miniature Horse colt named "Tiz Brave Heart". His photo in the ad showed a tiny fluffy foal playing with an open umbrella in the field while the other horses fled in fear. As soon as I saw him, I knew he was the one for me, despite an ad description of "special owner needed for this special colt" — which is horseman's code for "prepare for a challenge." Still, not wanting to rush into a big

commitment, I decided to wait three months before looking at his ad again, leaving it up to fate. I thought of him every day in that time, and when I saw that he was still for sale, I jumped at the chance.

His breeder informed me that he had nearly been sold in that time, with the potential owner having backed out the day before I called. It was meant to be.

As soon as this beautiful colt came into my life, he became known as "Willie" for short — and he is short, measuring in at 29 inches tall and weighing 174 pounds at maturity. During the winter, he looks like a tiny shaggy yak, but once that thick coat sheds out, he is the perfect equine model with his shiny black coat and white hind legs and tail.

Willie is a show horse born and bred, and there is no better place for him than in the show ring. When the audience claps for him, he'll spice up his performance, with no say on my part. He'll frequently canter and buck during the "trot up" in Halter classes, showing the judge (who is often holding back laughter) a heaping dose of pizzazz. In one Obstacle class at Old Home Week, for the final obstacle, he was supposed to place his front hooves onto a raised pedestal and stand for ten seconds. Having already witnessed his antics in the earlier class, the audience was ready for a show, and he gave them one. He approached the pedestal, looked around to great effect, and then dramatically placed one hoof at a time on it with a loud thud. He arched his neck proudly when the crowd cheered for him, and then he refused to step off it until he'd had his fill of the attention. Thirty seconds later. He took home a first place for that performance.

Because of his charisma, it was only natural that this small gelding would eventually acquire a fan club. There was a small group of people living in New Brunswick who made it a point to start attending all the miniature horse shows at Old Home Week on the Island after seeing him in action. They returned for three years in a row to watch the "littlest horse jump the moon." For those three years, Willie must have sensed them in the crowd, because he won the High Jump each time, setting a local record of a 44-inch-tall jump.

Willie now lives in Nova Scotia where he is a common local sight being taken out for walks in the village and strutting his stuff in parades. His softer gentler side has come out with the arrival of a regular herd of barn brats who come to visit him and his herd after school. He gets a lot of brushing, loving hugs, and kid secrets whispered into his tiny ears. He gives them an absolute run for their money when they bring him into the ring to practise. His cantankerous nature makes them work for results. Because of this, he brings out the light in even the shy children, building their confidence with every obstacle overcome and jump cleared.

"Prepare for a challenge," they'd said, but his talent all along was to prepare YOU for a challenge, wherever one arises in life. Just remember to follow Willie's lead and approach it with heart, spirit, and enthusiasm. Life returns it in kind.

# The Hair-Loving Kitty

Sharon Harris

# Ramsey

I t all began with an ending. When my father-in-law passed away, his second son, Julien, was left alone in the house they shared in east Vancouver. For Julien's birthday that year, his brother Terry (my ex-husband but still a very good friend) decided to get him a kitten to ease his loneliness. The kitten, a wee scrap of orange tabby, was selected the day before the birthday and spent its first night at Terry's house, curled up on my daughter's pillow, engaging in a pastime that mystified us from that day onward: chewing on hair. More will be said on that later.

At the birthday party the next day, the kitten was introduced to Julien who greeted the new arrival with tears and smiles. The bond was instantaneous and the two became inseparable. The kitten was named Ramsey — not a common cat name but very fitting as he proved to be a very uncommon cat.

During the ensuing years, Ramsey stole into our hearts with his quirky habits. All cats are curious, but Ramsey took that trait to new levels. His favourite perch was an inside window ledge in the living room, that allowed him an expansive view of his outdoor domain. Visitors to the porch were met with stares that said, "And who might you be?"

Once, when the window ledge was temporarily unavailable, Ramsey

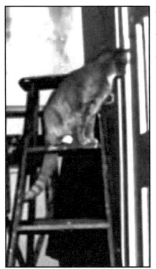

wailed with indignation. The interim solution was to place a step ladder in front of the high window on the front door. Peace was restored.

Ramsey loved hair. He would purr with contentment if he could sit on the back of the sofa and chew on your hair. I don't think he ate it. He just liked to get it all wet and yucky. Family members got used to this odd behaviour, but it was always a surprise for visitors, several of whom left with tufts of hair sticking out of their otherwise smooth coifs. I have since learned that for cats, this is a sign of affection, akin to grooming a friend. In the case of a kitten, it could arise from being weaned too soon.

Snap peas were another of Ramsey's peculiar loves. He took great pleasure in meticulously extracting the little peas from their pod and eating them. Dogs have treat puzzles. Ramsey had snap peas. Unfortunately, he wasn't as keen on the shells as he was on the peas so stepping or sitting on pea shells was always a hazard for visitors.

Sadly, we lost Julien to kidney disease and Ramsey was left alone in the house under the care of the downstairs tenant. This lasted for a few weeks while the house was emptied and made ready for sale. It was not a happy time for any of us, Ramsey in particular. Normally very playful, he became withdrawn.

At the time, I was living in a large condo rental. The owners were a lovely young couple, easy to get along with and flexible to my needs. However, my lease specified "no pets" so I was placed in an awkward situation when Terry and my daughter asked me to give Ramsey a home. No one else could take him and the alternative was to surrender him to a shelter. Having a pet was not something I had planned, but the thought of Ramsey in a shelter was too painful to bear. I laid out the situation to my landlords and they graciously agreed that Ramsey would be welcome as a room-mate — living rent-free of course.

Ramsey arrived the next week after being checked out by the vet. To my surprise, he came with a legacy from the estate that would cover all expenses for as long as he lived.

For three days, Ramsey hid under the cedar chest in the den. This should not have been a surprise as he was a thirteen-year-old cat that had known only one home. Nothing could entice him out, not even a supply of his beloved snap peas. His food remained untouched and his litterbox barely used.

Just as I was beginning to panic, he ventured out from his safe place. For the next day or so he wandered around the apartment, room by room, sniffing everything and exploring every nook and cranny but always returning to his place under the cedar chest. He finally decided that this was an acceptable home and curled up beside me on the sofa. That night he climbed up on my bed for the first time. I was hooked.

New home, new favourite food. From the day he moved in with me, Ramsey never ate another snap pea. It is as though snap peas were associated with Julien in his little kitty brain: no Julien, no snap peas. Instead, he developed an insatiable appetite for Safeway rotisserie chicken. Ramsey would always greet me enthusiastically when I came home, but if I were carrying a chicken carton, that greeting could only be described as ecstatic. He would purr, he would meow, he would reach up to me, he would weave between my feet rubbing against my ankles. I could only free myself by giving him a small dish of the prized delicacy.

About a year after Ramsey came to live with me, he was diagnosed with feline diabetes. I had never heard of such a thing and the next few weeks were some of the most trying I can ever remember. Understanding and living with this disease is very complex. It means frequent visits to the vet and a lot of learning. It means becoming proficient in testing for glucose levels and injecting insulin. None of this is pleasant for the cat and my heart ached for Ramsey.

The worst thing for me was the timing of injections. They have to be twelve hours apart. Not eleven hours, not thirteen hours. Twelve hours. That put a major wrench into my social life and I missed many an event or left early because I had to get home to give Ramsey his insulin. Most of the time, I took that in stride but sometimes it was hard. My frustration never lasted for long though. A furry cuddle was all I needed to put everything right again.

Diabetes is also very expensive. Test strips, syringes, insulin and vet visits are not cheap, and I was so grateful that Julien's estate looked after all these expenses.

A few months after Ramsey's diagnosis, I moved to a new apartment on the bank of the Fraser River. My tenth-floor view was nothing short of spectacular. I could see all the way to Mount Baker in the east, to the airport in the west, and many miles across flat farmland to the south. The Fraser is very much a working river and there were many things to see: tugboats, barges, lumberjacks working the log booms, pleasure boats and jet skis. I had a loveseat positioned close to the living room window and that became Ramsey's place. He would sit on the squishy top of the love seat by the hour, watching all the activity on the river.

He loved it all. This loveseat was getting up in years and because I wear a lot of black, the seat cushion had become increasingly discoloured. Not even professional cleaning could solve the problem and I yearned to replace it but could not deprive Ramsey of his own personal spot. The loveseat stayed.

My favourite time of day with Ramsey was bedtime. His advancing years meant it was harder and harder for him to jump up on the bed, so I placed a footstool on the far side of the bed and it only took him a few hours to figure out that this was his way up. Each night I would climb into bed and turn off the light. That was his signal. He would climb up, stick his head under the covers beside me, wriggle his way down to my knees, then turn around and wriggle his way back up to my shoulder so that just his head was sticking out. There he would stay for how long I never knew because by the time I awoke in the morning, he would be back on his loveseat. It was a wonderful way to fall asleep every night.

Just before the three-year mark of being diagnosed, Ramsey's diabetes went into remission. I did not know that such a thing was possible, and I don't believe it is for humans, but it does occasionally happen for cats. I was so happy that I no longer had to inflict the discomfort of testing and injections on him. Alas, remission can also signal that something even worse is happening and that was the case with Ramsey. He had developed cancer and crossed the rainbow bridge at age seventeen.

Alpha to Omega: beginning to end. Throughout his life, Ramsey brought joy to me and my family and I still think of him and chuckle whenever I'm preparing snap peas or enjoying a rotisserie chicken for dinner. I did eventually replace my old loveseat and while the new one is beautiful, it isn't perfect. It doesn't have Ramsey on it.

# Not the Booze, the Meow

Sherri Cariou

# Rumble

**R**umble came to us in response to an ad for his "temporary" care. According to the ad, the demands of having a new baby and moving to an apartment while the family was waiting for their new home to be built was proving too stressful. Having been there done that, it seemed only fair to offer help to both family and feline. After a quick family conference, and seeing how excited our two daughters were, we agreed to invite Rumble into our home for the requested six to eight months.

When the black twelve-year-old Rumble with half a tail was delivered to us, we expected that — like most cats — she would run and hide under a bed or some other safe haven until she was comfortable in her new digs. But not Rumble. She marched into the house with the attitude of "This will do fine."

It was readily obvious, that at a mere four pounds, Rumble was significantly underweight, with a noticeably shabby coat. According to her history, Rumble was a stray that had been found on the side of the road. We don't know if she was so named because of her very loud, exuberant meow, or after the rumble strip. Either way, the noise she made remains memorable.

Within a couple of months, Rumble — by then nicknamed Rum —

blossomed into a sleek six-pound ebony, happily thriving on the abundance of care and attention from our two daughters. Despite their growing attachment (and ours), we held fast to the agreement that the cat would be returning to its original family. Or so we thought.

During the first months of Rum's boarding with us, we received occasional updates from the original owner, but nothing firm about a collection date. As luck would have it, my partner spotted the original owner at a fundraiser where his attempts to chat were met with a blank stare. He reminded her that our family was caring for her cat. "The one with the half tail?" His enquiry as to when they would be ready to take the cat home was chillingly dismissive. She responded that their family and their other cat were nicely settled and that Rumble's return would upset their new lifestyle. She bluntly stated, that if Rum were to be returned, she would have her put down. With not a further word, my partner turned away in disgust. It seems we now had a cat.

By this time, it was June and the end of the school year. Although it was not our habit to give our girls grading gifts, we figured this was a reasonable exception. In preparation, we bought a new collar and tag with Rum's name and our phone number and handed this suitably wrapped gift to the girls. Their surprise was followed by the anticipated screams of delight. Rum now had a *furever* home — until her declining health compelled her to cross the rainbow bridge some years later, having lived her final years in relative luxury.

When we think of Rum, we do so with a smile at the joy she brought to our family. I'm often reminded of the day I called out to Rum while we had a repair person at the house. Not knowing the name was short for Rumble, the person said in surprise, "You've named your cat after an alcoholic drink?" I explained. As my daughter says, "If my parents were to name a cat after an alcoholic beverage, it would most definitely be called 'Wine'."

# Through the Lens of a Vet-Tech

recounted by Mikaila Cariou, RVT

# Ginger

I absolutely adored my parents' Husky that was around in my childhood years. Every birthday, Christmas and other occasion, I would ask for the puppy that never materialized. I also spent as much time as possible around dogs. I was convinced that I was a hardcore dog person. That is, until the day Ginger appeared.

Ginger, an orange tabby, was surrendered to the clinic where I worked when he needed emergency surgery to save his life. Afterwards, Ginger needed to be fostered until he was well enough to be adopted. Since none of my co-workers was able to take him, my family agreed to a short-term foster to allow his recovery. As is often the case, he never left.

I am grateful that my parents allowed me to keep him, even though I had to sign a "roommate agreement" for him to stay in his *furever* home. Not surprisingly, it didn't take long before he stole into each family heart.

When Ginger became my roommate, my sister and her bunny, Toby, were living with us. Since Toby-the-bunny had had a positive experience with a previous cat, he tried his hardest to be friends with Ginger by lying on the blanket beside him, inviting him to play and doing his best to socialize. Unfortunately, Ginger could not be enticed, demonstrating no interest in the attempted camaraderie.

Ginger is a linguist that understands quite a few words including "nap time". Say the word "nap" and he runs up the stairs to ready himself for his favourite pastime. His choice nap buddy — next to me, of course — is my dad. On one occasion, Ginger was nowhere to be found in any of his usual hiding places. We were concerned, so we contrived a plan to lure him out of wherever he was. I went through my routine of preparing my bag to go to the gym and my dad announced that he was "going to take a nap." Within minutes, there was Ginger lying on the bed acting casual as you please and pruning himself for the call to nap. We now know there is no need to panic. The word "nap" will bring him out from hiding.

If there's any truth to the adage "curiosity kills the cat", Ginger has certainly tempted fate. He is obsessed with paper bags, reusable shopping bags and other hiding places. Sometimes he gets his head stuck in the handles and walks around with this potential choking hazard trailing behind him and staring at us to set him free. Other times, he is found sleeping inside bags that are slated to be discarded. If a box is brought into the house, he hovers until the box is emptied and he is able to sit inside, peeking just over the edge.

Ginger has taught himself how to open cupboards so he can go in and explore. Unfortunately, he sometimes forgets how to get out and creates a commotion inside until one of us opens the door, only to have him spring out and scare the daylights out of us.

Ginger has proven to be a loyal companion and my best friend. He has been with me through thick and thin. Unlike many cats that ignore humans, he runs to the door when I arrive home and flops over for belly rubs, patiently waiting for as much attention as I can give him. It touches my heart because this is a greeting that Ginger reserves only for me. He also endures having his nails trimmed, his teeth brushed and being given medication when needed — totally without incident. But woe betide anyone else who tries!

It's often said that a "heart pet" or "soul pet" appears once in a lifetime, the pet that grasps your heart so tightly, the bond changes the way you live life. It becomes your soul mate, but in pet form. That's my Ginger.

Thanks to Ginger, I now consider myself a cat person. He is the best part of my day. Every day. I love him dearly and wouldn't trade him for the world.

# Tatl & Tael
## (aka The Naked Aliens)

As a lifelong lover of animals and a registered vet tech, I've met more than my share of pets, but the antics of Tatl and Tael are legendary.

Tatl and Tael, aka "the naked aliens" because of their hairless bodies, are ever so cute and the sweetest among cats. They live a very spoiled life, well-served within the household of my best friend, Brittany. However, when it comes to voracious appetites, none can compare to Tatl and Tael, not even the typically food-obsessed Labrador retriever — which says something!

If given the chance, these two will chew through plastic to get to the loaf of bread and then proceed to eat the ENTIRE loaf. Surely the taste can't be that appetizing to a cat. They also have an unprecedented taste

for medication, health supplements and have even swallowed an entire bottle of antibiotics. Obviously, the consumption of these items has gotten them into trouble but, fortunately, without any dire consequences. Tatl and Tael also joined forces to eat a bottle of RestoraLAX, the outcome of which is left to your imagination.

Now accustomed to the ongoing need for access control, Brittany's living space has become a veritable cat-proofed fortress. Child locks and other anti-intrusion devices have been installed to keep these two bandits safely at bay.

It seems to be working.

# Never Bet on My Horse Skills

## Gerry

Gerry is a Standardbred horse, trained for harness racing. However, when I met him, he was in the process of being retrained to "canter". This involves a three-beat stride rather than the two-beat movement used in harness racing. Gerry's owner bet that I wouldn't be able get Gerry to canter in both directions. Seems easy, right? Not so, because the three-beat movement would not have been normal for him. In fact, it was totally foreign.

As a naturally competitive person, I accepted the challenge. Gerry and I were successful, thanks in large part to Gerry's intelligence and cooperation. Thinking back, I'm sure I accepted the dare just for bragging

rights if I succeeded, but it was worth it.

As a result of our success, I started riding Gerry regularly. I taught him how to jump and I had the honour of accompanying him to his first shows. He turned out to be a truly awesome horse. We enjoyed several wonderful years together until Gerry

was purchased for a young rider and relocated to Prince Edward Island. Gerry now
enjoys regular exercise with his new rider and
is able to luxuriate in the expanse of a
ninety-acre property.

# Two Rats & a Guinea Pig
## Zazu & Snoopy

The word "roommate" normally refers to a person, and my human roommate, Kayla, was definitely amazing. That fact notwithstanding, one of the perks of going into animal sciences/veterinary medicine is ending up at schools that not only allow animals, but also openly encourage their presence. Our "university" was a working farm with cows, sheep, mink, chickens, *et al*. Extra credits for milking cows and training sheep were a grand option. Within the boundaries of this animal friendly environment, small mammals were openly welcome in student dorm rooms.

Given this hospitable trend, my roommate, Kayla, chose a Guinea Pig that she named Piglet. In keeping with the rodent theme, I chose two rats that I named Zazu and Snoopy. The entertainment they offered after a hard day of study and farm activity was a definite stress buster.

Zazu and Snoopy loved all the snacks they could get their little paws on. At playtime, they would use the freedom from their cage wisely and did their utmost to get into just about everything in sight. They were especially fond of sneaking snacks of mine back to their cages for midnight munchies. I even caught them trying to carry whole oranges to the stash! Zazu was particularly clever. No matter where she might be in the room, she would jump into my hands at the sound of her name, irrespective of the distance. They were both very sweet and well-behaved. They were not alone. Some students also had pet rats that attended class, sitting in our hoodie pockets.

With five roommates sharing the same space, it was definitely a full house — or, more accurately, dorm room. It's a memory I wouldn't trade for anything. I'm so glad I studied in a place that allowed me to have such cool roommates.

# Bobcat Release

Training as a veterinary technician certainly has its perks, not the least of which was a school placement at a wildlife rehab facility. One of my favourite days on the job was when I was able to participate in a Bobcat release. Since there were several cats scheduled to be returned to the wild that day, we had to travel to several different locations across Nova Scotia to find safe locations away from people, but also relatively close to where each of the cats was originally found.

The most amusing part of the whole day was when we stopped at a gas station. The Bobcats were secured in large dog kennels in the back of the truck. Before any of us could intervene, a woman who was filling her vehicle suddenly ran toward the truck saying that she wanted to see the cute dogs. She got quite the out-of-this-world surprise when she came face to face with a Bobcat instead.

It was both heartwarming and spectacular to see the now-healthy Bobcats returning to their natural habitat. However, the look of shock on that woman's face was priceless. It brings a smile to my face every time I think of it.

# A Healthy Fear of Birds

For a number of reasons, I have a healthy fear of birds. During my training, I remember being warned that because birds don't have a diaphragm, simply holding a bird incorrectly can restrict its breathing and cause death. I would be horrified if I accidentally killed anything, so that information has made me just a teensy bit paranoid about handling birds. Nonetheless, sometimes it's unavoidable as a vet tech.

During a mandatory rotation at a wildlife rehab centre, I was tasked with retrieving this one particular Pigeon that was adept at terrorizing people. There were other and much larger birds on site — not the least of which were Geese, Eagles, Falcons and other Birds of Prey — all of which had their own attack techniques. However, none of them held a candle to the fear this one Pigeon could generate. He  would purposely scratch vehicles, bite anyone who came too near, and constantly break into places he was not allowed. Despite my ongoing success at finding him, it was not an easy task to retrieve him. Truth is, I was much more comfortable going into the Bobcat enclosure than cozying up to any of the feathered residents.

My fear of birds was sealed when an absolutely beautiful Macaw came into the clinic for a pedicure. Being new to the job, I stood by to observe.

As my co-worker began trimming the nails, the Macaw leaned forward, gripped the space between my co-worker's fingers, twisted the skin with a vengeance — and then "laughed". For me, this was the final nail in the coffin, so to speak, ending in a firm resolve on my part that an avian-specific practice was not in the cards for me.

# A Hamster that Became a Bunny

## Toby

When my sister, Lauren, was studying engineering at university, she was keen to get a small companion pet of her own. She thought that a hamster might be a good choice to keep her company and to cuddle during the long hours of study. To show their support, my parents gave her a pet-store gift card to help with the purchase. Then they made the mistake of going on vacation. I emphasize "mistake" because my sister and I had a long-standing reputation for bringing animals home while they were away. After all, what could they do if it was a done deal?

As luck would have it, instead of going to the pet store, Lauren spotted a baby bunny for sale on a buy-and-sell site. According to the ad, this bunny was one of several that had been raised for meat, but the

breeder's daughter had become too attached to the litter. To avoid any trauma, the parents decided to sell the bunnies as pets. Enter Toby, Lauren's new university roommate.

As a kit, Toby learned to play beer pong, a game that involves

 throwing balls into the beverage cups of an opposing team and, if successful, getting to drink the contents of that cup. Toby became a pro at socializing during these parties.

Now a senior, Toby lives a luxurious and carefree existence with Lauren in her new home. He has the run of the house and his very own bedroom, where he sleeps at night.

Toby the bunny. The best hamster ever.

# Jafar

Among the many pets I've had, the most unusual (so far) is undoubtedly Jafar, a crayfish. He wasn't the most exciting of pets. He didn't play fetch or roll over to have his tummy rubbed. Instead, he spent his days trying to catch the fish in his tank, but without success. I guess Jafar might have become a bit bored with the monotony of the fish tank as he escaped to seek out more exciting options.

There was no immediate panic since crayfish can live out of water for short periods. Our cat, Rum, was going nuts smelling the floor, but even those valiant search-and-find efforts proved futile. Jafar was simply nowhere to be found. On the bright side, Jafar obviously had instinctive survival skills. When his time out of water began to run out, Jafar found his own way back into the tank, which we then secured to avoid any further incidents. Given his skill as an escape artist, I wasn't anxious to suffer nightmares about this mini-lobster crawling onto my face in the middle of the night.

# Closer to Home

## William Caw

# Charlie Claw

Cats can be fickle and this ginger cat was no exception. He arrived at our door — from whence we do not know — sauntered in and took up residence.

My parents referred to the cat's refusal to leave as "a takeover". Consequently, he quickly became known as Charlie Claw. The name Charlie was that of a financier who was receiving lots of news coverage at the time for his ambitious takeovers. The name "Claw" is somewhat obvious, but it was also a play on words by adding the "L" to our family name. Kismet!

My father, John, did not favour cats, although he would never have allowed any harm to come to them. No doubt Charlie sensed that bogus disapproval and, in his wisdom, focused all his attention on cozying up to Dad. Charlie's first move to gain favour was to jump onto the arm of Dad's chair, purring loudly as he stared. It worked. Dad's response was, "If he has the courage to be that cheeky, he might as well stay."

Charlie's takeover was almost complete. Next step was to oust our Dachshund from his bed by the fire and then commandeer the dog's food bowl until he was gifted with one of his own.

Charlie Claw was also a force to be reckoned with. He would spend hours out in the garden, standing guard and clearing the space of small critters that dared roam into his territory.

Charlie also enjoyed lounging on the back fence, watching the world go by and enjoying the sunshine. One day, he took exception to a German Shepherd that was simply walking by on the street. Obviously, Charlie figured that his boundary extended well beyond the wall as he took off after the startled dog and chased him all the way back to his own home. He then returned, reassumed his sunning position and went back to sleep.

A few years later, Charlie Claw tired of his life with the Caw family and, without so much as a by-your-leave, took up residence with a family down the street. He was spotted from time to time, but Charlie never returned. Such is the life of a takeover mogul.

# Our Back-to-the-Earth Period

Diana Lariviere

# William's Wild Animal Selection

During our back-to-the-earth period, William and I purchased an old farmhouse on a two-hundred-acre property in Ontario, complete with barn and various out-buildings. It proved to be both a challenge and amusing, beginning with the very first question William, a born-and-bred city boy, asked: "When we move to this property, will there be bears and wolves and other wild creatures?"

As I stared in disbelief, I couldn't help myself and answered "No, William. When we're settled in, all you have to do is boot the computer, open the 'wild animal selection program' and you can make your choices among the animals available." I know. Nasty on my part. I should have been more understanding ... but the taunting was fun.

# Bees, Bears & Roosters

Illiam's long-time dream was to raise honeybees. Fortunately, one of the first people we met was Bill, a beekeeper, who graciously offered to not only provide us with a couple of starter hives, but also with ongoing instruction and support.

We made arrangements to collect the hives at dusk, which is when the honeybees return from their daily foraging and the hive population is at its fullest. We first taped all the gaps between the various "supers" that were stacked together to form the "hive". This was done to reduce the possibility of bees escaping through the tiny openings while in transit. We then loaded and tied the two hives into the bed of the ancient truck that we had purchased for just such farm activities.

Bill the Beekeeper cautioned us to drive very slowly and to avoid as many bumps as possible, so as not to irritate the bees, as well as to prevent the hives from falling over. As we drove through the countryside, everything went well until we came to a tiny village. Suddenly, vehicle lights appeared behind us, so William pulled over to the side of the road to let the vehicle pass. No such luck.

As soon as we pulled over to the side, the red-and-blue lights went on, there was a quick *blip* of a siren and the door of the vehicle began to open. It was the police.

The expectation in such an encounter is for the driver and passengers to stay in the car, roll down the window and wait for instructions. Since

we were carrying several thousand bees that would soon be more than a bit irritated by the bright flashing lights and the sound of the siren, we knew that waiting patiently was not an option. Fearing for the police officer's safety, William jumped out of the truck — complete in a beekeeping suit, head cover and all. To those unfamiliar with this outfit, it would look much like a hazmat suit worn as protection from a toxic spill. The Fates only know what the police officer might have been thinking.

As the officer continued to emerge from his cruiser, he yelled out to William, "Get back in the truck." At that, I wondered if a handgun would suddenly appear. No fear. Quick thinking William, with lots of personal experience in policing, stopped as directed, but responded with "I will get back in the truck, officer, but I feel compelled to advise you that there are thousands of bees in those two hives. They are all very attracted to loud sounds and flashing lights."

Recognizing the immediate danger, the police officer slid quickly back into his vehicle, turned off the lights and the siren, and opened the cruiser window about an inch.

A conversation then ensued, during which the police officer explained that he had pulled us over because there had been several break-and-enters locally and our extremely slow speed seemed suspicious. Like we were casing the joint. The police officer then drove away — with no more flashing lights and no siren.

Several weeks later, we were rewarded with our first jars of honey. As a token of our understanding for the roadside stop, William dropped by the police station with a jar of honey for the officer who had pulled us over. Since the officer in question was not on duty that day, William recounted the story to the Duty Sergeant who laughed out loud, with hand slapping enthusiasm. He accepted the jar of honey on behalf of the absent officer. No doubt there was quite a bit of ribbing in the lunchroom that week.

Things returned to normal for a while in our honeybee world until a bear tore into one of the hives that we had moved into the upper field behind the barn. Obviously, William had neglected to make the correct choices in the automated "wild animal selection program" when we first moved in.

The first hint of a problem was when a mass of irritated honeybees suddenly appeared around the house and barn. William donned his beekeeping suit and headed up to investigate. He arrived in good time to witness the bear sitting placidly amidst the pieces of the now completely shattered hive, happily munching on its favourite delicacy, the honeybees, and blissfully licking the honey off its paws and nails.

During this time, we also had chickens, with numerous roosters among the flock. However, there was one particularly beautiful rooster that was master of the yard. He was also very much aware of his handsome features and would strut about, showing off his stuff. Most of the chickens were smart enough to run for cover when the irritated bees began to appear, but as is often the case with an overly handsome dude, Mr. Rooster would not stoop to running away. Then the bees found him.

As we watched from the safety of the house, Mr. Rooster's strut became a shuffle, with one leg in the air, then the other, then his one wing fluttering, then the other. He soon recognized the wisdom of running for cover. No worries. Mr. Rooster survived the episode relatively unscathed and soon resumed his pompous presence in the barnyard.

# House Bats

The very thought of a bat conjures images of Dracula sucking the blood of his human victims to turn them into a semblance of the walking dead. Truth is, there are thousands of different species of bat, all of which are useful to the environment and not all of which are bloodsucking.

When we moved into our old farmhouse during our back-to-the-earth period, the siding was in very poor condition and would eventually be replaced. In the meantime, we had to tolerate the odd mouse, snake or other creature that appeared in search of shelter.

As we were lying in bed one night, there was a faint sound of *flap flap flap*, whereupon I said, "William, there's something in the room." William was tired and said I was just imagining things. Rather than get out of bed to investigate, I turned on the flashlight. There, with wings spread across the window curtain, was one huge black bat. Just my imagination, eh? Well, I must have a pretty good one since I had not only heard the sound but had conjured up an actual bat.

Fully armed with a wastepaper basket and a thin binder, William managed to cover the bat with the basket, insert the binder behind the curtain and slide all three down the curtain. With the bat secured, William headed to the back door, made sure it was securely closed and released the bat into the darkness of the night.

This was pretty much an ongoing occurrence until the new siding was installed. We just got used to it, with William becoming very masterful at

 the trap/slide/release technique.

Somewhere off in the distance, I'm pretty sure there was a Bats Only Bar where all the bats gathered together to share their stories over a beer about the amusing Bat-Man who kept capturing and releasing them.

# Squatters' Rights

We cheerfully inherited two elderly Geese that we named after one of our former Prime Ministers and his spouse: Brian and Mila.

Brian spent most of his day relaxing, eating and honking loudly, so was probably well-named. Mila, on the other hand, was both interested in and wary of her new neighbours. The cats avoided her completely. Their reaction was much like seeing someone coming toward you and crossing the street to avoid them. The dogs soon learned that Geese were not things to be chased or else retaliation would be swift and painful — by Mila, who defended the forever-lounging Brian.

Despite their initial interactions, Mila took a particular liking to Toby, our sweet, gentle Irish Wolfhound/German Shepherd mix. Toby loved to lie on the grass in the warm sunshine and Mila would settle beside him, tuck her legs beneath her to enjoy both the heat and the company.

One day, we watched as Mila waddled curiously back and forth along Toby's back. All of a sudden, she bit him in the hind quarters and Toby rose on all fours in one quick jump. We're not entirely sure what prompted the nip, but it might have been Mila's way to move him off the grassy spot she wanted for herself. In any case, a momentary glance passed between them and they settled back down together in friendship.

For anyone who is in search of a reliable security system, Geese are a great option. They are willing to work 24/7. They don't complain about shiftwork. They never ask for an increase in salary. They happily work for grain and otherwise forage for themselves on grass, roots, seeds — pretty much anything that grows. In terms of work ethic, if anyone or anything comes onto the property, Geese raise an horrendous row that demands your attention and scares the dickens out of the trespasser.

By way of illustration, military training frequently involves creating two teams who assume the opposing roles of "attack force" and "defence force". During one such exercise, the objective of the attack force was to break into the "enemy" compound. The attack force was confident that the "soft points" of the facility would be easily breached. Given their knowledge of the layout, it was just a matter of a quiet approach after dark. Obviously, the vanguard had failed in its intelligence gathering and was unaware that a defence member of the "enemy" team hailed from a farm — a Goose farm. As the attack force approached the enemy compound in confidence, a tremendous honking sound exploded into the night. Seems that, just after dark, a massive gaggle of geese had been released by the clever defence team into the compound. The mock attack was foiled.

# Raccoons on Board

Given our fondness for animals, William and I volunteered with a wildlife rescue group to foster baby animals until they were ready to be released back into the wild.

Baby animals often end up in the care of rescue groups after their mothers are killed by a passing vehicle or when the mothers are trapped and removed to another area. Without their mothers, survival of the babies is unlikely without human intervention.

We were advised that we would be receiving ten baby raccoons ("kits" or "pups"). To prepare for their arrival, we had to build spacious outdoor cages constructed according to specifications provided by the rescue group. William built two large cages, each of which would house five raccoons: one male (the boar) and four females (the sows). Each cage also contained a housing box mounted on an internal platform to allow the animals to get up and out of the cold and blowing snow.

When the raccoons arrived, they were all so tiny and ever so cute. Their cuteness is a temptation that can easily lead to their being tamed, thereby jeopardizing their ability to fend for themselves upon release back into the wild. Despite that allure, we were committed to following the rules. In brief, we were to house, feed and care for each group (known as a "Gaze"), without encouraging human contact. Our duty was to make sure they were ready for release and to improve their chances for survival in the wild.

The Gaze in one cage did extremely well. We named the "Boar", the male raccoon, Roy, after William's good friend and best man. Roy — the raccoon, not the friend — grew into a very, very large, well-developed boar, with an independent and forceful personality.

Roy's four sows accepted him, stayed behind him when we approached for feeding and cage cleaning, let him eat first and generally followed his lead. Roy would approach us without fear and even deigned to allow us to pet him — briefly and only on his terms. This evolution was wonderful to watch, giving us confidence that, when the time came, survival was a definite probability.

The Gaze in the second cage didn't do anywhere near as well, entirely due to the misplaced affection of the Boar's former human custodian. Regrettably, that person had succumbed to the raccoon's cuteness and had chosen to bring him into the house, where he was treated like one of the cats, including litterbox training. Although no malice was intended by the former custodian, Henry, as we called him, never developed the independence or attitude he needed to be successful in the wild.

The four sows that shared Henry's space would block him from eating and hiss at him to keep his distance. We even found Henry banned from the housing box and sitting on his own out in the cold. We resisted the temptation to bring Henry indoors in the hope that he would "find his footing", but that never happened. Instead, we built a separate, smaller box for Henry to provide him with protection from the elements.

Henry also developed some very strange personal habits that suggested a vet visit might be in order. The vet could find nothing physically wrong and was unable to offer any practical solutions. Despite all these challenges, Henry survived the months of captivity.

The day came when we received a visit from the rescue group and were given the release authorization.

Roy and his sows were the first to be released. We donned heavy leather gloves to grab each of them by the scruff of the neck and put them into carrying cages. We then travelled to one of the upper fields of our two-hundred-acre property, opened the cages and watched, both sorrowfully and happily, as they sped away to freedom. The sows never looked back, but Roy turned for one last look as if to say, "Thanks, guys." It was very satisfying.

A couple of days later, we went through the same routine with Henry and his less-than-congenial companions. As with the first group, the sows made a mad dash for freedom, but poor Henry showed no interest in leaving us. As helpless as we felt, we left Henry to his own devices, accepting that nature had to be left to take its course.

A few weeks later, two raccoons appeared in our big red barn, one of them looking surprisingly like Henry, but with a limp. The second was a female that, so far as we could tell, didn't react to noise of any kind. We surmised that she might be deaf. We didn't feed them or entice them to stay. Despite the lack of enticement, these two made the barn their home. We were fine with that. Given their respective disabilities, we figured it was the safest place for them to be.

# Annals of Time Past

Diana Lariviere

# Dog Sledding to School

Long — *long!* — before my time, my siblings, Linda, Raymond and Edgar, travelled to school by dogsled. They each had a dog of their own, with individual sleds. Linda's dog was not at all enthusiastic about these ar-duous daily runs and, given a choice, would have stayed home in the cozy comfort of its doghouse. Linda had a hard time getting her dog to "mush", but fortunately, there was a brilliant incentive available.

For reasons unknown, Linda's dog detested Raymond's dog. Since the two would wreak havoc if they got within a nose of each other, the solution was for Raymond and his dog to leave first, with Linda's dog taking off in hot pursuit. Linda's dog never accomplished its objective, but at least they all got to school on time. Same routine on the return trip.

# Wolf Escort

As caretaker of a hunting and fishing lodge, my dad was always vigilant about what was happening in the dense bush around us. During thunderstorms, Dad's concern was that a lightning strike would ignite a forest fire, so he would sit in the screened-in veranda and watch for signs of any rising smoke. Once the storm had safely passed, he would venture out, gun in hand, on a long walk to check out any known problem areas. On one such occasion, Dad was gone longer than usual, causing Mom to worry that he might not make it back by dark.

Dad was always careful to share his intended route with Mom — just in case — so Mom went to look down the road in the direction from which Dad said he would be returning. Since cell phones and walkie-talkies were still a fantasy of the future, making contact was a matter of shouting loud enough or of getting a good solid visual of the other person.

Mom put her hand up to shade her face for a better view and spotted Dad walking along at a leisurely pace. Mom motioned to Dad to "look behind". Without missing a step, Dad carefully glanced over his shoulder to see that he was being followed, at a respectful distance, by a beautiful wolf. It was odd to see a lone wolf, but it was not unheard of.

As Dad reached the house to join Mom — by now waiting within the safety of the screened veranda — Dad mounted the steps to join her. The wolf stopped, took one last look, snorted (much like a dog), then turned and slowly meandered back into the bush.

Wolves in the wild are not animals to pursue, taunt, hand-feed or antagonize. However, wolves are beautiful creatures that are nowhere near as vicious and unpredictable as depicted in Hollywood movies. That negative image is just a "bad rap". Dad's wolf escort was simply satisfying its curiosity and, sensing no danger from the human, offered no threat in return.

# Bear Sightings

Spotting wild animals around the tourist lodge and our house was normal. Generally speaking, they didn't bother us, and we didn't bother them. My dad's golden rule was, "No shooting within a two-mile radius." I think the animals might have spread the word among the various species because there was always something around. In deer hunting season, the hunters would often return empty handed only to see a deer standing in the yard, munching away on something and taunting them with its stare — but my dad's rule was enforced.

Our house was about two hundred feet from the main lodge where the cooking was done and tourists were greeted. At night, Mom and I would head over, long before Dad. I learned from Mom to keep on talking to let the animals know we were close by. That way, they kept their distance. Mom would point the flashlight in a semi-circle as we travelled the short space and, more often than not, eyes from something would gleam in the stream of light.

My childhood friend, Susan B, would often visit for a few days but she never quite got used to the wild-animal presence. One day, Susan started screaming, "There's a bear outside! There's a bear outside!" I went to the door to see what all the commotion was, and there, off in the distance, was a bear crossing the road. "It's only a baby bear," I said. This didn't mollify my irritated friend in the least.

# Coonie
## (short for "raccoon")

Wild animals had an admirable comfort level around Dad. They were never captured, caged and tamed. They would just draw near without fear, which is how a lost baby raccoon happened to spend his first summer with us.

Coonie roamed freely around the property, always keen to greet people. Although he did receive some food from us, my dad was of the view that it was critical to long-term survival for Coonie to forage for himself. Which he did.

Coonie was also house-trained in the sense that he knew his business had to be done outdoors, so he had pretty free access to our living space. With his little "hands", he was able to flip or twist various container tops and open screen doors to venture in and out as he pleased — talents that did get him into trouble on occasion.

Mom had to be vigilant if this little thief was around while she was cooking. Coonie was especially fond of her chocolate cake batter, so Mom would hand him the relatively empty bowl after the batter had been poured into a baking tin. Sometimes, he just couldn't wait and would snatch the bowl or grab an already filled baking tin, swiftly scurrying off before she could catch him. In spite of this naughtiness, Coonie was just too cute to raise her ire.

On one occasion, Coonie got into the car of one of the tourists and stole away with a bottle of pills. Only the open bottle was found, with a pill or two strewn on the ground. We thought for sure that this would be Coonie's demise because, by the time we became aware of the burglary, it would have been way too late to do anything for the raccoon. Fortunately, Coonie didn't seem to suffer any side effects. In all probability, he had not found the look or smell of the pills very appetizing and just discarded them. Unfortunately for the tourist, the loss of the medication meant he had to cut his vacation short and head home.

In the evening, Coonie would join the guys on the porch when they were having their evening beer. When supper was called, the guys would place their beer bottles back into the case; but the bottles were not always completely empty. Left on his own with the beer case, Coonie once drank up all of the dregs of the beer bottles. It probably wasn't a huge amount, but certainly more than enough for one small raccoon to get properly drunk.

Turns out, Coonie was not a happy drunk. Next day, Dad found him staggering around the yard, in a really nasty humour, biting, scratching and growling, very much not his usual placid self. My dad donned a pair of heavy leather gloves and deposited Coonie unceremoniously into a cage for the day, together with a large bucket of water. When Coonie was released, he was seen walking a few steps and then taking his

"hands" and rubbing the sides of his head — the discomfort resulting from one massive hangover.

Coonie stayed the summer, surviving all his little adventures. In the autumn, a rather attractive lady raccoon appeared to tempt the now-handsome, burly male that we had come to cherish. They hung around together for a short while, with Coonie's new admirer maintaining a respectable distance from Coonie's human friends. Fortunately, Coonie had been encouraged by Dad to be independent so, when love and hormones took hold, Coonie chose the call of the wild. We missed him terribly, but we knew he was where he belonged.

# Squirrelly

Squirrels are common in the country and with some encouragement, this little squirrel grew to trust my dad. Not only would the squirrel eat from Dad's fingers, Squirrelly, as he became known, would run up and down Dad's pantleg and collect treats from my dad's shirt pocket.

Now, one point of note is that, because Dad travelled through the bush on a daily basis, he had developed the practice of tucking his pantlegs into his boots and then lacing up the boots around the pants. This allowed Squirrelly to travel up and down Dad's leg without any risk of entry up the inside of the pantleg.

Along comes a teenager — I'll call him Max — who was fascinated with this "trick" that my dad had taught Squirrelly. Unfortunately, Max was wearing Bermuda shorts and sandals — all loose and airy.

Yep. Having been taught the trick, poor ol' Squirrelly didn't distinguish between Dad's pantleg and the bare "leg" of any other. Without warning, Squirrelly, sprang across the ground and up Max's pantleg… but there was no way out. Squirrelly shuffled around a bit and came down the OTHER pant-leg.

It all happened so fast, there was little could be done. Max turned whiter than a sheet and stood so still, we thought for sure he was going to collapse on the spot. Max survived. Meanwhile, Squirrelly scampered off into the nearby trees, looking forward to looting my dad's pockets another day.

# Closing Notes

I hope you have enjoyed reading the stories and loving memories of all our beautiful animals as much as all our contributors have enjoyed writing about them.

Many of our stories reflect the need for greater emphasis on animal welfare and more education on the wide range of animal needs. Financial support is a huge requirement, but giving animals a "voice" to be heard by those who are responsible for decision-making in the political arena is absolutely key to improving the life of animals. To that end, we offer you the "references and suggestions" included herein. The wide range of animal welfare issues is sufficiently complex that some of the following information might come as a surprise.

## No Such Thing as a FREE Pet

*"Keep in mind*: there is no such thing as a 'free' pet. Oftentimes, there's a hidden reason why the pet was offered for free. Sometimes that reason has to do with its current health status — from relatively simply things like barn cats that are flea infested or, in the extreme, puppies with serious parvovirus. Even when healthy pets are offered 'free to a good home' from the current owner or from a veterinary clinic following a surrender, the pet will require vaccinations, regular health checks and perhaps expensive surgeries, especially as they age. Although we love each and every

companion that comes into our lives, pets are not 'cheap'. Be willing to open your heart and offer a good, loving home … BUT, prepare for the financial reality. Pet health insurance is highly recommended to alleviate costs over the long term." — Mikaila Cariou, RVT.

# Abandonment, Abuse and Cruelty = Criminal Offence

Mistreatment of animals in any form is a criminal offence under the *Criminal Code of Canada*, sections 445 to 447.1.

https://www.princeedwardisland.ca/sites/default/files/publications/royal_gazette/rg_issue_4-january_22_2022.pdf

Few people, including those responsible for administration of these sections of the Criminal Code, are sufficiently well-versed in its content, meaning or application. Asking lots of questions, including, "Why? Where is that written? And what's your legal reference?" are highly recommended, regardless of the source of information.

The wording of the animal-related sections of Canada's Criminal Code is weak, thereby allowing offenders to escape punishment.

Provincial/territorial laws in support of the Criminal Code of Canada vary significantly, contradict each other — even within the same jurisdiction — and are not consistently applied.

A national organization called Animal Justice (created by Camille Labchuk, BA, JD) identifies itself as "Canada's only national animal law advocacy organization." Animal Justice focuses on "overhauling the legal system to better reflect our country's values of compassion and justice for all."

https://animaljustice.ca (or search "animal justice Canada")

An overview of the shortcomings of Canada's animal laws is available online:

https://youtu.be/_pnDut48UCg

(Or, search using the phrase "overview of animal welfare legislation", or contact Animal Justice for info on access.)

# Animal Abuse, Abandonment or Cruelty — What to Do if You Suspect It

Personal intervention in the moment is high risk, may be dangerous to you and should normally be avoided.

Regrettably, the laws and policies vary among jurisdictions — and sometimes even within the same jurisdictions — and research on what to do may take time while the animal continues to suffer. Be prepared. Conduct that research in anticipation of possibly needing it.

### Places to Contact

- Local animal shelters and rescue groups. Not all of these are authorized to intervene, but they usually know whom to contact.
- The municipal office for name/title/contact information of the designated authority. You might have to inform them of their obligations under the *Criminal Code of Canada*.
- The police force responsible for your area. However, they might have to be reminded of their authority and obligations under the *Criminal Code of Canada*.
- Your MP, MLA and Municipal Counsellor. These individuals are essentially your "employees". You elect them with your vote and you fire them with your vote. If they are interested in remaining in office, they should be willing to assist you in finding the correct information.

### For Advice in Extreme Cases:  Animal Justice

https://animaljustice.ca

## Animal Groups — What to Expect

The best and most highly respected animal welfare organization in the entire world is Battersea, in the United Kingdom. Few, if any, of the Canadian animal welfare organizations meet the Battersea standard. This website provides all types of information and checklists.

https://www.battersea.org.uk/about-us

# Animal Welfare Groups — How to Differentiate among Them

The terms HS (Humane Society) and SPCA (Society for the Prevention of Cruelty to Animals) are often used interchangeably, but they do differ. Although many of the local HS/SPCA are members of national Canadian organizations, operational practices may vary from one region to another.

Similarly, the terms "shelter" and "rescue" are often confused. "Shelter" usually indicates that the organization has a building in which to house rescued or surrendered animals, whereas "rescue" organizations often operate though a system of fostering animals in the homes of their volunteers.

*Shelters* — whether HS, SPCA or locally established — do not all operate under the same principles and policies. For example, some sanction euthanasia to reduce over-crowding, while others are "no kill". An Internet search using a phrase such as "animal shelter checklist" will provide useful questions to local organizations not only to determine their legitimacy, but also whether their philosophy is in line with your personal beliefs.

Sample checklist (but there are numerous others):

https://www.aspcapro.org/resource/shelter-checklists-based-asv-guidelines

*Rescue* — The vast majority of animal rescue organizations operate in the best interest of the animals; however, some "rescue" organizations are alleged to be scam fronts for "puppy mills". As with all things: Beware.

Regardless of the claims that might be made on a website, a social media page or other "ad", one concrete way to determine the legitimacy of an animal welfare organization is to ask for detailed financial records. Don't settle for a "financial statement" that lumps expenditures under general categories. Be "forensic". Before donating, insist on information that clearly lists all sources of income and details of how money is spent.

## Animal Welfare — How to Increase Awareness

- Review this "Animal Justice" video for suggestions … *The Rise of Animal Rights Law in Canada: Why You Don't Need a Law Degree to Play a Part.* https://www.youtube.com/watch?v=_pnDut48UCg (If you are unable to access the video, contact Animal Justice to request it.)
- Sign the various petitions that are online. Search "animal petition". Petitions alone do not normally change the law, but they do raise awareness. *Beware*: There are several "fake" petitions online. Take the time to read the small print AND check out the alleged "source" (originator) of the petition.
- During elections (whether municipal/provincial/territorial/federal/ other), raise the issue with candidates. Make it an election issue. Follow up regularly on progress. And ask those around you to do the same. Remember the saying "The squeaky wheel gets the grease."
- Support "LEGITIMATE" animal welfare organizations by volunteering or offering financial support. However, do your own

research to confirm that their practices are compatible with your expectations and your beliefs. Similar to buying goods: Supporter, beware.

- Never doubt that a small group of thoughtful, committed citizens can change the world; indeed, it's the only thing that ever has." — Margaret Mead, anthropologist, recipient of the Planetary Citizen of the Year Award in 1978.

# Animals in War — Remembrance Day, Awards & Recognitions

Countless animals — dogs, horses, pigeons and yes, even at least one cat, and other species — were conscripted into every war in human history. Sadly, many of these animals died, were injured and — even worse — were left behind to fend for themselves or to become food for starving inhabitants. It's only relatively recently that military personnel have insisted on bringing their animal comrades home safely. In recognition of animal service, several countries commemorate animal participation in several ways, including (but NOT limited to): The Dickin Medal (the UK's animal equivalent of the Victoria Cross).

https://www.pdsa.org.uk/what-we-do/animal-awards-programme/pdsa-dickin-medal

### Animals in War Memorial (UK)

https://www.royalparks.org.uk/parks/hyde-park/things-to-see-and-do/memorials,-fountains-and-statues/animals-in-war-memorial

### Purple Poppy (Australia)

https://www.purplepoppies.com.au/

# Canine Blood Donations

Did you know that your healthy dog can donate blood to save other animals? To find out more OR to register your dog as a donor:

- conduct an Internet search using the phrase "dog blood donations"; or
- contact a nearby veterinarian for information on a collection outlet near you.

### One of numerous examples: Canadian Animal Blood Bank:

https://www.canadiananimalbloodbank.ca/

# Cats and Kittens — Q & A

- How many litters can a female cat (aka the Queen) produce in a year?

    The gestation period for a cat is about two months; therefore, the average is four litters per year. However, the Queen can *potentially* produce five litters per year.

- How many kittens could be produced in each litter?

    The average litter is three to five kittens, but there can be as many as ten kittens in a litter.

- How many kittens can the Queen potentially produce in a year?

    On the HIGH side: five litters per year × an "average" of five kittens per litter, for a potential total of twenty-five kittens per year, *per* un-spayed female cat.

- How many stray, abandoned and otherwise unwanted cats/kittens end up in shelters?

    Lots. Contact shelters and cat rescue groups in your area to obtain statistics.

- How many stray, abandoned and otherwise unwanted cats/kittens are euthanized?

    Lots. Contact shelters and cat rescue groups in your area to obtain statistics.

- At what age a cat should be spayed/neutered?

    The recommended age varies for a myriad of reasons. A major concern is that cats can become pregnant as young as five months old, so under five months is often suggested so as to prevent unwanted kittens. However, there are also concerns about pet health and bone development that suggest waiting longer. The best source of advice is the nearby veterinarian that you plan to choose as your practitioner.

- How much does it cost, per year, to own a healthy cat, including one-time spay/neuter, annual rabies and other injections, food and when-necessary veterinary visits?

    These costs will vary, based on where you live and which veterinary practice you choose. A nearby veterinarian is the best source for estimates on veterinary care. A nearby pet food store is a good source for estimates on food and other comfort costs.

## Children and Animals — Expectations

Sharing your life with an animal can be both fun and rewarding, but both parents and children need to understand, accept and commit to the responsibility required to invite that animal into your life.

A quick search of the Internet using phrases such as "teaching children about animals" will provide reams of information, hints and guidelines. As a start, THE KEY POINTS are that the dog, cat or other animal:

- is a lifetime commitment, sometimes as much as fifteen or twenty years. It is not a toy to be discarded when the novelty wears off or its needs interfere with other human activities, or it begins to age;

- may be an expensive undertaking to cover initial vaccines and spay/neuter, as well as ongoing treatment and medication to maintain good health;

- requires more than just food, water and a warm bed. It needs exercise and as much attention as a human child or an elderly relative does; and

- deserves respect and should never be expected to tolerate a child's bad behaviour — no matter what the age of a child. He/she is "just a baby" is no excuse for causing pain or distress to the animal.

  In extreme cases, this type of behaviour may actually be a warning sign. Studies reveal that the vast majority of convicts who tortured, abused, maimed, killed or mistreated people began their criminal careers by practising on animals. (Internet search using "serial killers and animal cruelty".)

# Choosing the RIGHT Dog

This is a personal choice. Some people favour one particular breed and always choose that breed when their current fur-baby crosses over the rainbow bridge. Others (like me) favour rescue, irrespective of the breed or mix. That said, there are some cautionary notes:

### Breed Specific

- Movies are notorious for popularizing a particular breed, resulting in increased purchases of that breed. However, each breed of dog has characteristics that are peculiar to that specific breed. Regrettably, these breed-specific characteristics are often not compatible with the lifestyle of the person/family making the purchase. Accordingly, it's in the best interest of the purchaser to:
  - research the breed characteristics through a reliable source, such as the Canadian Kennel Club. https://www.ckc.ca/en;

- consider your personal and family lifestyle;
- understand the difference between "purebred" and "pedigree" (see separate section); and
- research the legitimacy of the breeder to ensure the dog is not being purchased from a "puppy mill", a questionable "backyard breeder" or a "front" rescue organization.

## Rescue

- understand the difference between and among the various shelter operations and rescue groups (see separate section);
- some are imported from regions that have ailments and diseases that don't exist in Canada. Their acquisition can spread the disease and be expensive to treat;
- be patient. Be prepared for the possibility of a challenge. Some of these dogs have never lived in a house and are not house-trained. Some have been abused and are wary of humans. Some are suited for adults, but not for children; and
- to end up with a better dog, invest in an experienced trainer who practises "reward" to encourage the dog to cooperate. Avoid trainers who incorporate "punishment" (including prong-collars; shock collars, etc.).

# Choosing a Suitable Dog Trainer

Your choice of dog trainer will depend on your own personal beliefs. Generally speaking, successful dog training requires time, lots of patience, rewards and repetition — lots of repetition. No matter what advocates of shock collars, prong collars or other punishment techniques might promote, there are no short cuts.

For a list of suggestions, search the Internet using the phrase "choosing a dog trainer" and myriads of sites will appear, such as this one: "Companion Animal Psychology".

https://www.companionanimalpsychology.com/2016/12/how-to-choose-dog-trainer.html

# Dogs and Puppies — Q & A

- How many litters can a dog produce in a year?
  Most female dogs go into heat about twice per year, with the approximate gestation period being 58 to 68 days; therefore, the maximum number of litters would be three per year.
- How many puppies could be produced in each litter?
  The average litter is five to six puppies; but there can be as few as one or as many as twelve.
- How many puppies can a female dog potentially produce in a year?
  On the "HIGH" side: three litters per year × an "average" of six puppies per litter, for a potential total of 18 puppies per year, *per* un-spayed female dog.
- How many stray, abandoned and otherwise unwanted dogs/puppies end up in shelters?
  Lots. Contact shelters and dog rescue groups in your area to obtain statistics.
- How many stray, abandoned and otherwise unwanted dogs/puppies are euthanized?
  Lots. Contact shelters and dog rescue groups in your area to obtain statistics.
- At what age should a dog be spayed/neutered?
  The recommended spay/neuter age varies. Dogs can become pregnant at a very young age, so early spay/neuter is often recommended in an effort to prevent unwanted puppies. However, there are also concerns about pet health and bone development that suggest waiting longer. The best source of

advice is the nearby veterinarian that you plan to choose as your practitioner.

- How much does it cost, per year, to own a healthy dog — including one-time spay/neuter, annual rabies and other injections, food and when-necessary veterinary visits?

    These costs will vary, based on where you live and which veterinary practice you choose. A nearby veterinarian is the best source for estimates on veterinary care. A nearby pet food store is a good source for estimates on food and other comfort costs.

# Emergency CAT Rescue Kit

We all hope that our cat will never go missing; however, cats are curious creatures or the confusion that arises during emergencies or natural disasters can all contribute to the cat's being lost. It's worth being prepared with a "kit" of relevant, useful items (or copies thereof) to keep in the "Kitty-Cat-Kit", including:

- photos: full front head, plus side and back views. Keep these photos current, as cats may change in appearance with growth and age;
- name and detailed description of the cat — especially any unusual markings — as well as any notes about behaviour and disposition, even though these may vary if the cat is under duress;
- microchip number. This is painless and well worth the cost of the implant. For cats that may look similar, the implant also alleviates arguments over ownership, something a cat collar cannot do. As a precaution, have your local veterinarian record the microchip number in the cat's health records;
- current health record, including vaccination certificates, just in case the cat has to go to a shelter or kennel;

- a list of medications, with a small supply thereof. But make sure the supply is kept "fresh";
- spay/neuter certificates. Critical if the cat happens to wander into a different jurisdiction;
- contact information for local shelters, rescue groups and others to make them aware the cat is missing;
- blanket, a bottle for water, a supply of cat food, a light-weight food dish;
- a small litterbox (even a collapsed cardboard box with a few plastic bags will do);
- a bag of litter; and
- other items as may come to mind or as recommended.

# Emergency DOG Rescue Kit

We all hope that our dog will never go missing; however, a loud noise — especially during fireworks displays — or the confusion that arises during emergencies or natural disasters can all contribute to the dog's being lost. It's worth being prepared with a "kit" of relevant, useful items (or copies thereof) to keep in the "Dog-Emergency-Kit", including:

- photos: full front head, plus side and back views. Keep these photos current, as dogs change in appearance with growth and age;
- name and detailed description of the dog — especially any unusual markings — as well as any notes about behaviour and disposition, even though these may vary if the dog is under duress;
- dog licence number. This is available from your area Municipal Office or its designate. Usually at a relatively low fee;
- microchip number. This is painless and well worth the cost of the implant. For dogs that may look similar, the implant also alleviates arguments over ownership — something a dog collar cannot do.

As a precaution, have your local veterinarian record the microchip number in the dog's health records;

- current health record, including vaccination certificates, just in case the dog has to go to a shelter or kennel. Best to consider "kennel cough" in regular vaccination updates. Just in case;
- a list of medications, with a small supply thereof, but make sure the supply is kept "fresh";
- spay/neuter certificates. Critical if the dog happens to wander into a different jurisdiction;
- contact information for local dog shelters, rescue groups and others to make them aware the dog is missing;
- blanket, a bottle for water, a supply of dog food, a light-weight food dish;
- adding a tag, or burning your current telephone number into the dog collar that the dog usually wears, is also recommended;
- a roll of doggie-waste bags, just in case you find yourself in an area that requires waste pick-up;
- other items as may come to mind or as recommended.

# Financial Assistance for Pet Acquisition and Medical Expenses

Non-profit organizations that provide financial assistance for pet acquisition and spay/neuter are available in many areas.

- Financial assistance depends on income and usually requires the cat-owner or would-be cat-owner to submit an application for assistance.
- There are also some national and international non-profit organizations that provide a range of animal-related financial

assistance. These normally require more-substantial and detailed written submissions.

- Virtually all of these non-profit organizations operate through fundraising by volunteers — and are always in need of more volunteers — as well as bequests via wills.

# "Purebred" versus "Pedigree" — What's The Difference?

These terms are often used interchangeably, yet they are very different. According to Canada's *Animal Pedigree Act*:

https://laws-lois.justice.gc.ca/eng/acts/A-11.2/

- *pedigree* means genealogical information showing the ancestral line of descent of the animal;
- *purebred* means an animal that is a purebred of the breed as determined by the by-laws of the association authorized to register animals of that breed.

The term "pedigree" is very well monitored and overseen by the Canadian Kennel Club (CKC):

https://www.ckc.ca/en

… and its subsidiary organizations. The CKC is incorporated under Canada's *Animal Pedigree Act*.

The term "purebred" is a bit more complex. In simple terms (subject to your own research and your own enquiries directly to the CKC), the term means the offspring of two dogs of the same breed. There are many reputable breeders who focus on producing "purebred" puppies rather than "pedigree" and these caring, reputable breeders ensure their female dogs are not overbred and, more to the point, they guarantee the health of the puppies that are produced under their watch.

Regrettably, the word "purebred" is the favourite term used by "puppy mill" operators, as well as by "deceitful" backyard operators. These are persons who overbreed, who accept payments and then don't deliver the puppies, who sell inter-bred puppies that develop all sorts of ailments and who have no conscience about selling unhealthy puppies. These shady, devious operators throw a terrible and unwanted shadow on legitimate, caring breeders of purebred puppies, while taking advantage of well-meaning, caring buyers.

A quick Internet search will reveal a ream of suggestions and information on how to identify (or at least be wary) of potential "puppy mills" and deceitful backyard breeders. Pay attention to the myriad of cautionary notes. Contact the CKC and/or its affiliates to identify legitimate breeders. As with any purchase: Buyer beware.

## "Reputable" Breeder — What to Look for

An Internet search using a phrase such as "signs of a good dog breeder" will provide a mound of information.

But the various sites agree on:

- You will be invited to meet the puppy and the parents; or, as a minimum, the mom;
- they don't advertise on buy-and-sell sites;
- they don't ask for money "up front" before meeting the puppy;
- you will have to sign an agreement to have the puppy spayed/ neutered and to return the puppy to the breeder if you no longer want or cannot keep it; and
- they usually belong to a known kennel club.

# Acknowledgments

Writing this book has been much more of a challenge than I would have expected. The stories have been rolling around in my head for a long time, but putting those words on the page in a readable story format has been a huge undertaking. This "writing" stuff is real work!

It can also be a very discouraging exercise. It requires a lot of encouragement and support to keep going — and plenty of networking. I am amazed at how many people I needed and am overwhelmed at how many of those individuals offered their support to help me … from start to finish. To each and every one of you, no words would sufficiently express how grateful I am — but let me make a valiant attempt.

- My coast-to-coast review team, Sharon Harris (British Columbia) and Peggy MacLean (Nova Scotia), who so generously dedicated so many personal hours to reviewing the stories, highlighting the various faux pas, correcting the grammar, pointing out discrepancies and making every story so much more readable. I could not have come this far without you.

- My longtime friend and go-to person on technical issues, Dr. Lynn McMullin-Robblee, DVM, who patiently answered my many veterinary-related questions and sorted me out on so many things. I just hope I understood correctly and got it right in the text! Any errors or omissions are entirely mine. (Maritime Veterinary Holistic Services. http://calmvet.com/)

- My amazing contributors who graciously shared their own heart-warming stories — both happy and sad — to add to the book's variety. Each of you has made this journey so much more exciting and I hope that my rendition does justice to the "tails":

  - Mikaila Cariou, RVT (Nova Scotia),
  - Sherri Cariou (Nova Scotia),
  - Line Decarie (Québec),
  - Sharon Harris (British Columbia), and
  - Abby Sawyer, Author; Artist, Small Cat Studies (https://www.facebook.com/smallcatstudios); owner, Panfer Gold Farm (https://www.facebook.com/PanferGoldFarm); and new mom (where does she find the time!).

- Patti Larsen, author extraordinaire who, despite the numerous demands on her own schedule, took time out to share so much useful information and to encourage me to move forward. (https://www.pattilarsen.com/)

- Sherrill Wark, author, editor, graphic designer and long-time friend, who supported me from start to finish, who ignored my moments of resistance and who nudged me over the finish line to completion. (http://crowecreations.ca/)

- My long-suffering husband, William Caw, who tolerated my long hours of writing, my moodiness when things weren't going well and my short-temper when things really went belly-up. Were it not for him, I would not have remained well fed — with the occasional martini (shaken, not stirred!) waiting for me on particularly challenging days.

- Last, but not at all least, I would be remiss in not thanking my faithful and constant companion, Gizmo, who lay quietly under my desk during the long hours of writing, re-writing, swearing and editing. More importantly, he never failed to remind me that it was time for a break — including a long-luxurious walk to the beach to meet up with his doggie pals.

# About the Author

Diana Lariviere currently lives in Argyle Shore, Prince Edward Island, overlooking the Northumberland Strait. There she shares the fabulous view, beach and rural setting with her husband of thirty-plus years, William Caw, and their amazing dog, Gizmo.

Diana has written countless technical documents, mostly human resource policies and practices, as well as arbitration decisions that had the potential to be submitted for judicial review. Over the years, Diana has also written social columns for several newspapers in Ontario and Prince Edward Island, as well as short stories and articles for several magazines and publications. She is well-known among friends and family for her cheery and chatty annual "newsletters". This is Diana's first non-fiction publication written just for fun.

Diana owes her inspiration for this book to her current fur-baby, Gizmo. He was adopted from the Lillian Allbon Animal Shelter, Mamas Last Litter Program (https://www.laanimalshelter .org/mamas-last-litter), located just across the Confederation Bridge, in Amherst, Nova Scotia. This shelter promotes a unique program that

encourages low-income families to bring accidental or unwanted litters to the shelter for adoption. The resultant adoption fees are then used to have the mother spayed by a qualified veterinarian.

Gizmo's mom was a Parson Russell Terrier and his dad was a German Shepherd, both mixed with whatever else. No one knows for sure. That parental blend has given Gizmo a unique look — so much so that passersby frequently ask, "What breed is he?" After becoming weary of the question, Diana's tongue-in-cheek answer became, "He's a Japanese cattle dog."

Now that a breed had been clarified, establishing a "pedigree" was an absolute must. After two days of deep contemplation, they came up with "Gizimoto Heindrich Kobe of the Osaka Line". The embarrassing part was when this very tall tale was shared (with a smile), some folks said, "Oh, yes. I've heard of those!" It was way too embarrassing to openly admit there is no such thing.

Diana and Gizmo have shared lots of training: puppy, obedience,

rally, basic agility … and lots of practice. Although Gizmo is quite swift, his human is not, so agility remains "fun" only. Because verbal commands are integral to training, Gizmo's comprehension skills are exceptional and probably exceed that of any country's top politicians.

Gizmo has become quite popular with the summer-cottage dogs and their human com-

panions. During walks along the country road, he is readily recognized for going into a "sit" as soon as he sees a car coming. That elicits a smile from all but the most avid non-dog people.

Gizmo has also become known within the community for his participation in Remembrance Day Ceremonies at which he lays a wreath for "animals of war". His participation is raising awareness of the need to recognize animal contributions and sacrifices.

39707314R00103